Ian Thomas specialises in the law relating to food and non-food consumer products.

He is a dual qualified lawyer practising in England and Wales and in the Republic of Ireland.

Ian advises on all aspects of food law and practice including new product development, general compliance issues, enforcement actions, appeals and prosecutions, as well as representing clients in courts and tribunals.

He works with clients in the UK, Ireland, Europe and globally and as a barrister he accepts instructions directly from clients under the Bar's Public Access Scheme.

Ian presents at lectures and seminars and he provides practical skills training to non-lawyers on matters such as evidence gathering and preparing to go to court. He is a consultant trainer with La Touche Training.

Ian is an elected Fellow of the Society of Food Hygiene and Technology.

He is a member of the following organisations; Food Law Group, the Certification Committee of Excellence Ireland Quality Association, the Food Safety Professionals Association, the Course Committee of the Food Regulatory Affairs and Veterinary Public Health programmes at Ulster University and University College Dublin, the Institution of Occupational Safety and Health, the Bar of England and Wales and the Law Society of Ireland.

A Practical Guide to
The Law Relating
to Food

A Practical Guide to The Law Relating to Food

Ian Thomas LL.B (Hons), FSOFHT
Member of the Course Committee of the PgC/PgD/MSc Food
Regulatory Affairs and PgC Veterinary Public Health programmes
at Ulster University and University College Dublin
Barrister at Law – Chambers of Stephen Hockman QC,
6 Pump Court, London
Solicitor, Republic of Ireland, Ian Thomas Associates
Food and beverages, non-food consumer products,
licensing and health and safety

Law Brief Publishing

Published 2018 by Law Brief Publishing, an imprint of Law Brief Publishing Ltd
30 The Parks
Minehead
Somerset
TA24 8BT

www.lawbriefpublishing.com

Paperback: 978-1-911035-75-6

For Aisling and Ciara

PREFACE

It hardly needs saying, but food law is a vast subject area.

This book contains a practical guide to the regulation and enforcement of some of the more common areas of food law. Of course, what are "common areas" depends on the food law adviser's own practice and no doubt topics of interest to some readers are not included. This is due to pressure of space and staying true to the original brief of producing a short, user-friendly general and practical book.

This book will, hopefully, be relevant for experienced practitioners, students in food related subjects and others with no more than a passive or active interest in the subject.

Food law, like all other areas of legal practice depends on legal rules, but it also requires an understanding of people and advising on, and solving, problems in the "real world". As such this is deliberately not a detailed legal text book, although law is of course referred to throughout.

Food law covers all stages from primary production to the product that appears on the supermarket shelf, or internet web page, and hence what ends up on our plates. It is everything "from farm to fork" or from "conception to consumption" and applies to all stages in between.

Food lawyers may be involved in litigation, or we may become part of corporate and commercial work advising on the regulatory and compliance issues applicable to the merger or acquisition of a food business.

We may also be asked to advise on a range of other issues relating to new product development, in connection with labelling or claims, nutrition, processing techniques, general compliance issues, pursuing or responding to actual or threatened enforcement action and finally to acting as advocates in the criminal or civil courts.

We need to know a little about the history and development of EU law, but much more about the substantive provisions of EU food law and how to interpret them as well as the application of them in a domestic law context. We need to understand that food is a global commodity and hence we need to be able to advise on the law of local markets or to facilitate the provision of such advice.

Food business operators need to sell their food in a manner that is compliant with a wide range of obligations but want to appeal to consumers by marketing it in the most commercially advantageous way.

Food lawyers need to understand how the food industry operates and the challenges facing individual clients, but also to have a sense of how the competent authorities are likely to respond in any given situation. Clients range from start-up enterprises to well established food businesses to large national and multi-national establishments, as well as competent authorities at national and local level.

Food law is substantially based on rules enacted at European Union level. It is then given effect in each Member State and, as applies in the UK, with some differences within that Member State.

I have therefore concentrated on the EU law aspects of the various topics contained in the book but the chapters on enforcement, prosecution and sentencing inevitably have a "bias" towards the law and practice of the UK. There may be some interest in a book that looks at matters from a more Ireland-specific perspective or which focusses on certain topics in more detail, or this may be my one and only publication of this size!

I cannot leave the preface to a food law book without mentioning the future and the UK's departure from the European Union. People in the UK, the EU and around the world will be affected to a greater or lesser degree by Brexit. Although the impact of some issues is becoming clearer, many uncertainties remain. Everyone should plan for the impact of Brexit and take steps to minimise and adverse consequences this may bring. This issue is discussed further in chapter 10.

I would like to thank everyone who has helped, supported and motivated me throughout my career both in the UK and Ireland; family, friends, food professionals (lawyers, scientists, advisers and consultants), colleagues inside and outside the legal profession and, finally, to the barristers, clerks and support staff at 6 Pump Court.

I also wish to thank Tim Kevan and Garry Wright of Law Brief Publishing for allowing me the opportunity to write this book which I hope is informative and interesting as well as being enjoyable (in so far as a law book can be "enjoyable"!).

Any comments or observations made in the book are personal and do not necessarily reflect the view of others. All errors in the text are mine and mine alone.

The law is stated as at 20th April 2018.

Finally, as Albert Einstein supposedly said, if you can't explain it simply, you don't understand it well enough. Having practised in regulatory law, and food law in particular, for quite a long time I will leave it to you, the reader, to decide whether I pass that test.

Ian Thomas
April 2018

CONTENTS

CHAPTER ONE
GENERAL PRINCIPLES
OF FOOD LAW

Introduction

This chapter will consider some of the general principles of food law including how food is regulated at European Union level and at national level along with some of the main concepts set out in Regulation (EC) No 178/2002 (the General Food Law Regulation or GFLR).

Background

Adulteration, often with hazardous substances, and misdescription of food and drink have been the scourge of consumers and legitimate food businesses for a very long time.

Legislation alone cannot provide the answer but it can set rules for what is prohibited and what punishment can be expected by those who fail to comply.

An early example of this can be seen in the Adulteration of Coffee Act 1718 (5 Geo. 1 c. 11) which provided a penalty of 20 pounds

> "*against divers evil-disposed persons who at the time or soon after roasting of coffee, make use of water, grease, butter, or such like material whereby the same is made unwholesome and greatly increased in weight, to the prejudice of His Majesty's Revenue, the health of his subjects, and to the loss of all fair and honest dealers.*"

In the following century, scientists and others identified many examples of adulterous and misleading practices and were not afraid to "name and shame" those responsible. One of the early pioneers of this work was German chemist Frederick Accum whose lengthy and informative work, A Treatise on Adulterations of Food and Culinary Poisons, was published in 1820. Accum identified, uncovered and publicised the widespread problem of food and drink adulteration and his efforts were followed by Thomas Wakley and Arthur Hill Hassall. Their innovation, along with the development of scientific techniques and the creation of the public analyst service, greatly helped in the detection of these illegal practices and sowed the seeds for a modern framework of food law and regulation.

While history often helps to inform modern thinking, for the purposes of this book, a useful starting point for a general understanding of current food law and regulation is the European Commission's White Paper on Food Safety dated 12th January 2000 (COM (1999) 719 final).

The White Paper followed a number of high profile food crises including BSE in cattle and the Belgian dioxin contamination of animal feed in 1999 and was published when the time was ripe for the creation of a co-ordinated and integrated approach to food safety and best practice in responding to food crises. All stakeholders have an important role to play in adopting a system that regulates food along the entire food supply chain; from "farm to fork" or from "conception to consumption". The White Paper, on page 3, announced a "radical new approach" to "guarantee a high level of food safety".

The White Paper led to the creation of the European Food Safety Authority (EFSA) and the enactment of the General Food Law Regulation, arguably the lynchpin of modern food regulation.

Current food regulation in the European Union and in Member States

Current food law is based on a mix of European Union law (Regulations, Directives etc.) and national law (Acts of Parliament, Statutory

Instruments etc.) supplemented, where necessary, with rules from Codex Alimentarius, Codes of Practice, guidance and case law.

At EU level, the two main pieces of legislation come in the form of Regulations and Directives.

An EU Regulation is "binding in its entirety and directly applicable in all Member States"; the same law applies throughout the EU. Member States are left to enact laws giving effect to the Regulation and dealing with ancillary matters such as enforcement and punishment for non-compliance.

A Regulation may empower Member States to adopt their own rules on certain aspects of the legislation (see for example the provision of food information in respect of non-prepacked foods contained in Article 44 of Regulation (EC) No 1169/2011).

A Directive on the other hand is "addressed to the Member States" which then enact national laws giving effect to the object and purpose of the Directive. Where this creates divergence and uncertainty between the food laws of Member States there may be an impact on intra-EU trade.

EU laws can be found in many places, one of which being the "Eur-lex" website. This can be used to research legislation, identify amendments thereto and see a list of relevant case law.

EU food law is enacted following a process that involves the Parliament (the peoples' representatives), the Commission (the EU "civil service"), the Council (ministers from the Member States), the Court of Justice of the European Union (interpreting EU law) and the European Food Safety Authority (providing advice on scientific issues).

EU law has to be relevant to and have regard to the 500+ million EU citizens with their differing needs, requirements, language, culture and history. This can result in a law based on compromise which the national institutions must then interpret, apply and enforce.

Interpreting EU law requires a careful assessment of the wording of the legal provision but also, and of particular relevance for food law, by having regard to the context in which the law occurs and the objectives pursued by the rules of which it is part (see for example *Merck* Case 292/82, and *Verband Sozialer Wettwerb eV v Innova GmbH* Case C-19/15). This often means going beyond the mere "letter of the law".

For further reading in relation to interpretation of hygiene laws in an EU context see the decisions of the Court of Justice of the European Union in, *Albrecht and others Case C-382/10, 6 October 2011* (containers for self-service retail of bread and bakery products) and *Astrid Preissl Case C-381/10* (the installation of a washbasin in food premises). They are discussed further in chapter 3.

In a national context within the UK, the High Court has confirmed the above position concerning interpreting EU law; "when interpreting these [food hygiene] Regulations, it is necessary to have regard to the purpose for which they were created, namely, to protect consumers with regard to food hygiene." (*Kothari, Naik and Raw Lasan Ltd v London Borough of Harrow [2009] EWHC 1354 (Admin)*)

Where the national court is concerned with the interpretation of a particular EU law, or particular wording within it, the matter might be referred to the Court of Justice of the European Union for a preliminary ruling under Article 267 of the Treaty on the Functioning of the European Union (TFEU). The Court of Justice will then provide a decision on the correct interpretation and the case returns to the national court which will resolve the issue in dispute having regard to the decision of the Court of Justice. This does not mean that the national court must slavishly follow the CJEU's ruling.

A recent example of the interaction between EU and national law can be seen in the case of *R. (on the application of Newby Foods Limited) v Food Standards Agency* concerning the interpretation of relatively short, but commercially and practically very important, provisions of Regulation (EC) 853/2004 on the hygiene rules for products of animal origin.

That case has been the subject of numerous hearings in the High Court and Court of Appeal (see [2017] EWCA Civ 400) in addition to the ruling by the CJEU. At the time of writing, early 2018, an appeal to the Supreme Court is pending.

Other general EU principles which are relevant to the food lawyer include the Precautionary Principle under which action may be taken where a food is potentially dangerous but where the risk has not been fully determined. The principle of Subsidiarity means that the EU may only take action when the objectives of the proposal cannot be sufficiently achieved by the Member States; i.e. an EU-wide response is required. The principle of Proportionality means that EU actions may not exceed what is necessary to achieve the objects of EU rules; this is also very important in the context of the interpretation and application of EU and national rules, particularly in the area of enforcement.

The extent to which food law, regulation and enforcement will be affected once the UK exits the European Union is the subject of much speculation and indeed some degree of concern.

A final point should be made about current food law and regulation within the UK. Care must be taken to identify the appropriate competent authority having jurisdiction over the particular product or activity. This includes matters of policy and responsibility for enforcement.

Mutual Recognition

Food is an international commodity and as such the food business and its advisers need access to competent local market advice. While the law may be the same or similar, it is important to ascertain what the trading conditions are like "on the ground" and how the laws are regulated and enforced by the competent authorities.

In an EU context, the principle of mutual recognition provides that a product lawfully produced or marketed in one EU country may be sold in other Member States without being subject to financial or other barriers.

This arises from the creation of the internal market and the general prohibition on imposing restrictions on imports and exports within the European Union (see for example, Articles 26, 28 and 30 of the TFEU).

Member States may not create rules which amount to "quantitative restrictions" on the movement of products (see Articles 34 and 35 of the TFEU).

However, prohibitions may be imposed on grounds of "the protection of health and life of humans, animals or plants", but this must not amount to a "means of arbitrary discrimination or a disguised restriction on trade between Member States" (see Article 36 of the TFEU).

Any attempt to go behind the free movement of goods must be justified, proportionate and for the benefit of consumers.

When assessing the impact of a particular restriction, regard must be had to the product itself and whether or not there are any EU-wide harmonised rules regarding the composition or labelling of the product which apply in the Member States.

For further reading about the principles of mutual recognition, reference may be made to, *Procureur du Roi v Dassonville v S. A. ETS Fourcroy and S. A. Breuval et Cie, Civil Parties (Case 8/74) [1974] 2 C.M.L.R. 436* (Scotch Whisky)*; and Rewe-Zentral AG v Bundesmonopolverwaltung für Branntwein (Case 120/78) [1979] 3 C.M.L.R. 494* (French liqueur, 'Cassis de Dijon') and *EC Commission v Spain (Case C-12/00) and EC Commission v Italy (Case C-14/00)* (chocolate).

The General Food Law Regulation – Regulation (EC) 178/2002

The General Food Law Regulation (GFLR) contains some of the key building blocks of knowledge for a wider understanding of current EU food law and how it should be interpreted and applied. Specific matters covered in the GFLR include, unsafe food (Article 14), traceability (Article 18) and the withdrawal or recall of food hazardous to consumers (Article 19). These issues are covered in later chapters.

The General Food Law Regulation – some basic concepts

Scope (Article 1) and general application (Article 4)

The twin principles of the GFLR are; "a high level of protection of human health and consumers' interests in relation to food", and "ensuring the effective functioning of the internal market".

The Regulation applies generally to all stages of production, processing and distribution of food, and also of feed produced for, or fed to, food-producing animals.

Food (Article 2)

The definition of food (also described as "foodstuff") is:

> *"any substance or product, whether processed, partially processed or unprocessed, intended to be, or reasonably expected to be ingested by humans".*

This includes; drink, chewing gum and any substance incorporated into the food during its manufacture, preparation or treatment, but excludes; feed, live animals (unless prepared for placing on the market for human consumption), plants prior to harvesting, medicinal products, cosmetics, tobacco, narcotic or psychotropic substances, and residues and contaminants.

Objectives (Article 5 and Article 8)

The main objectives of food law include; a high level of protection of human life and health and the protection of consumers' interests, including fair practices in food trade. Food law should allow consumers to make informed choices in relation to the foods they consume.

Food business operator (Article 3 and Article 17)

The food business operator (FBO) is "the natural or legal persons responsible for ensuring that the requirements of food law are met within the business under their control".

Establishing the identity of the correct FBO is a matter of law and fact. Questions of control and/or the extent of control over particular aspects of the food business may be important as the FBO is usually the person against whom enforcement action is taken.

The FBO may be a company and/or an individual, and as was said at paragraph 21 of the judgment in *The Queen on the Application of Rasool v Tower Bridge Magistrates' Court [2013] EWHC 4736 (Admin)* "it is clearly right that it is possible in law for there to be more than one FBO".

Food law (Article 3)

This means the laws, regulations and administrative provisions governing food in general, and food safety in particular, whether at Community or national level; it covers any stage of production, processing and distribution of food, and also of feed produced for, or fed to, food-producing animals

Food business (Article 3)

This is any undertaking, whether for profit or not and whether public or private, carrying out any of the activities related to any stage of production, processing and distribution of food. The concept of "undertakings" in food law is based on an assessment of the degree and level of organisation of the activities.

Each situation is different and detailed instructions should be obtained but it is likely that somebody who handles, prepares, stores or serves food occasionally, on an ad hoc basis and on a small scale may not be deemed to be an "undertaking" (see for example, paragraph 3.2.1 of the Food Standards Agency's Food Law Practice Guidance (England) 2017). This may include a one-off event in a village hall.

This issue is particularly important to determine whether registration is required, see below, but even if it is not, those in charge must still take steps to protect the safety of the food they are making and/or selling.

Stages of production, processing and distribution (Article 3)

The definitions of food law and food business refer to obligations at any stages of production, processing and distribution. This means;

> *"any stage, including import, from and including the primary production of a food, up to and including its storage, transport, sale or supply to the final consumer and, where relevant, the importation, production, manufacture, storage, transport, distribution, sale and supply of feed".*

Hazard and risk (Articles 3 and 6)

The GFLR states that food law is based on risk analysis. This combines risk assessment, risk analysis and risk communication.

A hazard is "a biological, chemical or physical agent in or condition of food or feed with the potential to cause an adverse health effect" and risk is "a function of the probability of an adverse health effect and the severity of that risk, *consequential to* a hazard" (my emphasis).

There must therefore be a hazard before there can be a risk; an important concept when advising in respect of food safety and food hygiene.

Placing on the market (Article 3)

This is much wider than a mere sale or supply and is defined as;

> *"the holding of food or feed for the purpose of sale, including offering for sale or any other form of transfer, whether free of charge or not, and the sale, distribution, and other forms of transfer themselves".*

The phrase can be seen in the prohibition in Article 14; "food shall not be placed on the market if it is unsafe".

Rapid alert system (Article 50)

This is a system "for the notification of a direct or indirect risk to human health derived from food or feed". This is part of the Commission's emergency planning and crisis management to protect consumers from harm. It is particularly beneficial to warn consumers in several Member States that a food has been identified as hazardous to their health.

Pre-market notification or permission

Businesses

In general terms, a food business will either register with the competent authority (e.g. a restaurant registers with the local authority in whose area the business operates) or it requires approval from the competent authority (e.g. a slaughterhouse requiring approval from the Food Standards Agency).

Registration is done by completing a food business registration form which is often available on-line. This tells the competent authority, the local council for example, that the business is operating and provides information about the activities taking place (what type of food is being sold, is it mainly prepacked or is on-site production taking place). The FBO does not have to wait for permission before it can start trading. The business must thereafter notify the authority if there is "any significant change in activities" or if the business closes down (Article 6 of Regulation 852/2004 on the Hygiene of Foodstuffs).

The authority will add the business to its list of food premises which it will inspect in accordance with its own policy. The frequency of inspection being related to the level of risk created by the type of activity taking place (a small retailer selling mainly prepackaged food is likely to have fewer hazards and therefore a lower risk profile than a large restaurant business or large retailer making food on site).

Food businesses that handle products of animal origin are usually required to obtain prior approval from the relevant competent authority (e.g. the FSA). This is a formal process in which the FBO, its premises and its activities are inspected and only if everything is in order will approval be given. The FBO cannot begin trading unless and until approval is given which may be conditional or final.

Businesses that only need to register may have very infrequent contact with officials from their competent authority. However, business requiring approval may be supervised by Official Veterinarians (OVs) who are present whenever the activities are taking place (e.g. slaughtering of animals) and the OV may report issues of non-compliance as and when they occur; sometimes on a daily basis.

<u>Products</u>

Unlike some consumer products, medicines for example, food does not generally require a licence, authorisation or permit before it may be placed on the market.

However, the legislation should be carefully checked and by way of example, EU legislation provides for the pre-market notification of certain products and this will depend on the law in a particular Member State.

The EU law on food supplements provides that a Member State may require the FBO to notify the competent authority before a supplement is placed on the market. A food supplement may not be placed on the market in Ireland unless the FBO has sent a notification, including copies of the product labels, to the Food Safety Authority of Ireland. The FSAI will review the form and the label and may, but is not required to, notify the FBO if it identifies a problem and/or it may liaise with other competent authorities (for example with the Health Products Regulatory Authority if the product is making medicinal claims). Similar pre-market notification provisions do not apply to food supplements in the UK.

Irrespective of any requirement for notification or pre-market contact with the competent authority, responsibility for ensuring compliance with food law rests with the FBO.

Conclusion

A solid understanding of the basic principles of food law is essential for those who are new to the area and also for established practitioners to avoid falling into the trap of "familiarity breeds contempt".

Going back to basics and checking the actual legal definitions contained in the GFLR can be useful when asked to advise on a food law issue. This may be particularly useful when identifying the correct food business operator, reviewing the concepts of hazard and risk, and defining unsafe food.

Establishing a network of trusted food law advisers within the EU and in other local markets will help the food business expand and diversify its trading opportunities. With the onset of Brexit, this is more important than ever.

CHAPTER TWO
FOOD SAFETY

Introduction

Food safety issues are often caused by or contributed to by poor hygiene practices and therefore the next two chapters cover these two very important separate, but very much related, topics.

Issues relating to food safety are important to a proper understanding of other food law issues particularly relating to the food business operator's (FBO) obligations to take action to protect consumers from hazardous foodstuffs (e.g. withdrawal and/or recall – see chapter 6).

Although this chapter sets out the provisions in relation to unsafe food, Regulation (EC) No 178/2002 (the General Food Law Regulation – GFLR) imposes a similar provision in respect of feed in that Article 15 states: "feed shall not be placed on the market if it is unsafe or fed to any food-producing animal if it is unsafe".

Investigations involving alleged unsafe food may engage the services of the Public Analyst, despite their dwindling numbers, the Government Chemist or other appropriately accredited laboratories or suitably qualified experts. Samples taken from food, humans, premises and animals might need to be analysed and the results explained.

In every case where legal proceedings are taken or contemplated, all parties should have regard to the rules around sampling and all appropriate evidential rules, particularly in relation to gathering, recording, handling and transferring of samples and other evidence.

Although it may appear "obvious" that a foodstuff was unsafe and "must have" caused an illness, the party asserting this must be able to prove this to the appropriate evidential standard and the other party should check and test the evidence presented by the competent authority or an individual consumer.

References to Articles in the remainder of this chapter are to the General Food Law Regulation unless expressly stated to be otherwise.

Food safety (Article 14)

Article 14 (1) is quite blunt; "food shall not be placed on the market if it is unsafe".

The term 'placing on the market' is broader than sale or supply (see chapter 1).

<u>Unsafe food (Article 14 (2))</u>

Food is deemed to be unsafe if it is considered to be injurious to health and/or unfit for human consumption.

<u>Determining unsafe food (Article 14 (3))</u>

In determining whether any food is unsafe, regard shall be had:

(a) to the normal conditions of use of the food by the consumer and at each stage of production, processing and distribution, and

(b) to the information provided to the consumer, including inform-ation on the label, or other information generally available to the consumer concerning the avoidance of specific adverse health effects from a particular food or category of foods.

A couple of points may usefully be made here.

Raw meat is, usually, unsafe to eat. The 'normal conditions of use' have regard to the need to cook meat properly in order to remove the hazard.

Article 14 (3) (b) might apply to a food containing an ingredient causing an allergy or intolerance.

Injurious to health (Article 14 (4))

In determining whether any food is injurious to health, regard shall be had:

(a) not only to the probable immediate and/or short-term and/or long-term effects of that food on the health of a person consuming it, but also on subsequent generations;

(b) to the probable cumulative toxic effects;

(c) to the particular health sensitivities of a specific category of consumers where the food is intended for that category of consumers.

Article 14 (4) (c) might apply to a food that is marketed as being suitable for coeliacs but which contains gluten.

Unfit for human consumption (Article 14 (5))

In determining whether food is unfit for human consumption, regard shall be had to whether the food is unacceptable for human consumption according to its intended use, for reasons of contamination, whether by extraneous matter or otherwise, or through putrefaction, deterioration or decay.

Unfitness might equate to food being "unacceptable" perhaps due to extensive mould or to unexpected organoleptic properties such as strong taints, odours or tastes, or food containing hair, a plaster or a fingernail.

Depending on the type and/or quantity of the extraneous matter, the same food might be both injurious to health and unfit for human consumption.

Food in a batch (Article 14 (6))

Where any food which is unsafe is part of a batch, lot or consignment of food, it is presumed that all the food in that batch, lot or consignment is also unsafe, unless following a detailed assessment there is no evidence that the rest of the batch, lot or consignment is unsafe.

Where the competent authority has shown, after proper sampling and analysis, that some of the food is unsafe, it can then rely on the presumption that all the food is unsafe. Unless the food business operator (FBO) samples and analyses other products from the batch and shows they are not unsafe, the whole consignment is likely to be detained and destroyed.

The FBO must consider their options carefully and the response will depend on all the circumstances. If the problem has been traced to an unsafe ingredient that the FBO knows has been used in all the food in the consignment, there may be little point in obtaining costly analysis in order to try and displace the presumption. As consumer safety is paramount, the FBO often faces an uphill struggle to persuade the competent authority, or a court, that the presumption should not apply.

The financial value of the consignment, the shelf-life of the product, the cost and resources required to test product and the need to fulfil a particular order may be relevant to how the FBO responds to the consignment being detained because some food has been shown to be unsafe.

Food in compliance with specific Community provisions (Articles 14 (7) and (8))

Food that complies with specific Community provisions governing food safety shall be deemed to be safe insofar as the aspects covered by the specific Community provisions are concerned.

It should be noted that Article 14 (8) allows competent authorities to take action to impose restrictions on a food being placed on the market or to require its withdrawal from the market where there are reasons to suspect that, despite such conformity, the food is unsafe.

Any decisions or action would have regard to the need to protect con-sumer health and would only be taken following a detailed risk assessment of the food.

Practical application – a case of food poisoning

Consuming unsafe food may lead to serious illness and, possibly, death.

The consequences for consumers will depend on a variety of factors including their age and general health, the source and cause of the illness and the amount of the harmful pathogen that has been con-sumed.

Investigating, prosecuting and defending food poisoning cases in the criminal and civil courts is not always straightforward. In every case a thorough and detailed enquiry must be made by all parties. Evidence to prove, or disprove, liability is required and sometimes it is necessary to look beyond what might, at first glance, appear to be the 'obvious' cause of the problem. Nothing should be taken for granted.

The following issues may be relevant issues to be investigated and proved.

• <u>The source</u>

  The contamination may be due to salmonella, Escherichia coli (E. coli) or norovirus.

• <u>The cause</u>

  Food can become contaminated at any stage of production, pro-cessing or cooking. For example, it could become be contaminated due to incorrect cooking, handling, storing or reheating. Food consumed past its "use-by date" could be the culprit. The food could have become contaminated from within the food premises but any contamination could have occurred after it had been purchased by the consumer.

- Symptoms

  Symptoms may be minor (some pain and sickness resolving within a day or two, with or without medical consultation/intervention), moderate (where the symptoms are worse or more extensive and lasts for days requiring medical intervention), severe (leading to more extensive medical intervention, such as hospital admission) or fatal (where death is caused by or contributed to by having consumed the unsafe food).

- Notification to the food business operator

  The FBO might become aware of the problem in many ways; direct contact from consumers and/or the competent authority which may provide specific information about the problem (e.g. when the alleged food poisoning occurred, the possible 'suspect' foods, who was affected etc.) and this may assist the FBO to investigate the situation. Alternatively, initial knowledge may come indirectly via social media which can make the situation more difficult to manage.

  The FBO will immediately carry out their own investigation and take such steps as are necessary to protect consumers (e.g. by destroying or quarantining all the 'suspect' ingredients in a restaurant pending further investigation and obtaining new supplies).

  The FBO may need to undertake urgent works such as a deep clean of the premises and equipment, reviewing its food safety management system, revising it where necessary, and retraining staff.

- <u>The investigation by the competent authorities</u>

Investigating a food poisoning outbreak may involve multi-disciplinary meetings at which all the relevant agencies (e.g. food authorities, public health organisations, health protection teams and medical practitioners) will identify and monitor the scale and extent of the problem. This may involve communicating with consumers, other competent authorities, FBOs and health professionals. In a widespread serious case where speed of notification of the risk to consumers is important, this may require communication via television, print media, the internet and social media.

The investigation may involve taking samples from:

- People who have been ill (e.g. stool samples);

- From the suspect food (if it is available or from food from a similar batch, if possible);

- From the food premises (e.g. from equipment used to prepare the food or work surfaces); and

- Possibly from animals (e.g. if it is suspected that the initial source of the contamination occurred at a farm or market).

The aim is to try and identify a common source, including the particular strain of the pathogen, linking the illness with a particular FBO, food or food premises.

The complainants may be asked to complete a food history questionnaire which records information about the food they had consumed over a period of time prior to the onset of illness.

The aim of the investigation is to try and identify a particular food or foods and/or location common to all the complainants.

The FBO(s) under suspicion will be spoken to by the officials from the competent authority as part of the evidence gathering process and the FBO will wish to cooperate with the investigation. However, it is important that the FBO seeks legal advice early in the investigation and take guidance about how they interact with the relevant authorities, particularly if the FBO, or members of staff, are being questioned or, much more importantly, if they are requested to attend an interview under caution during which the competent authority will seek to obtain evidence for use in court proceedings.

- Legal action

  The competent authority may take action to immediately close the premises which are suspected to be implicated in the food poisoning, or example by means of Hygiene Emergency Prohibition Notice and/or to detain foods (see chapter 7).

  After a full review of the evidence, the authority may decide to bring criminal proceedings and/or the injured parties may bring civil actions seeking damages for personal injury. Both of these may be very costly for the FBO and some, but not necessarily all, of the financial outlay may be covered by suitable insurance.

- Some other points to note

  Any legal proceedings must be based on the sufficiency of admissible evidence (e.g. from complainants, environmental health officers, health professionals, scientists and other experts) to prove the case to the appropriate legal standard of proof ("beyond reasonable doubt" in a criminal prosecution and "on the balance of probabilities" in civil proceedings).

  During the official investigation, the officers should keep all their work under review to ensure that they are obtaining all the relevant evidence and doing so in the correct way. This might include taking samples, continuity of obtaining, storing, handing and transmitting evidence, correct use of the caution when questioning FBOs and others, using competent, appropriate and accredited laboratories and obtaining evidence from everyone who is involved in the case.

If this is not done at the appropriate time during the investigative process it may not be possible to 'fill any evidential gaps' later on. If there are gaps then this will be identified and exploited by the defendant and their advisers.

Conclusion

Food safety is very often linked to poor hygiene practices. Food information is also relevant to keeping consumers safe by providing information about ingredients, correct procedures for cooking and storing food and by the correct application of use-by dates.

In summary, when advising on food safety issues, including food poisoning cases, never take anything for granted, challenge everything (within reason and only when appropriate to do so) and always bear in mind that the cause of any illness may not be due to fault on the part of the FBO or the evidence may not be sufficient to prove fault.

CHAPTER THREE
FOOD HYGIENE

Introduction

The main EU food hygiene rules are found in Regulation (EC) No 852/2004 on the hygiene of foodstuffs (hereafter in this chapter 'Regulation 852') and Regulation (EC) No 853/2004 on specific hygiene rules for food of animal origin (hereafter in this chapter 'Regulation 853').

In addition, Regulation (EC) No 2073/2005 on microbiological criteria for foods is relevant as a means of checking the suitability and acceptability of foods and processes. It lays down food safety criteria for relevant foodborne bacteria, their toxins and metabolites, such as Salmonella, Listeria monocytogenes, Enterobacter sakazakii, staphylococcal entero-toxins and histamine in specific foods. It also lays down certain process hygiene criteria to indicate the correct functioning of the production process.

Definitions in other food legislation are relevant when applying food hygiene rules and this can be seen from Article 2 (2) of Regulation 852 which states, "the definitions laid down in Regulation (EC) No 178/2002 shall also apply" (and see similar provisions in Article 2 of Regulation 853).

Arguably the most common interaction between food law and criminal law involves prosecutions for breach of food hygiene regulations (which may or may not include prosecutions for placing unsafe food on the market – see chapter 2).

Food hygiene cases are likely to receive media attention particularly where the food business is well-known or where there is some "interesting" element to the case which often involves evidence about the presence of rodents in the food premises.

In addition to prosecutions, food hygiene issues feature highly in relation to the grounds for taking enforcement action such as issuing as Hygiene Emergency Prohibition Notices (see chapter 7).

Hygiene of foodstuffs – the general rules – Regulation 852/2004

Food hygiene rules are intended to ensure a high level of consumer with regard to food safety in three main ways:

1.   Legislation to prescribe minimum hygiene standards;

2.   Effective official controls to check levels of compliance by food business operators; and

3.   The creation, operation and maintenance of appropriate food safety management systems and procedures based on Hazard Analysis and Critical Control Point principles (HACCP).

(See for example, Recitals 7 and 12 of Regulation 852).

In addition to the Recitals, from the practitioner's perspective there are three key, but interrelated, parts to Regulation 852:

1.   Chapter 1 – the general provisions;

2.   Chapter 2 - food business operators' obligations; and

3.   The Annexes

Regulation 852 can be described as imposing the following main obligations:

1.   Primary responsibility for compliance rests with the FBO (Article 1 (1) (a));

2.   The Regulation applies without prejudice to more specific requirements relating to food hygiene (Article 1);

3.   The FBO must "ensure that at all stages of production, processing and distribution of food under their control satisfy the relevant hygiene requirements laid down in this Regulation" – obligations from "farm to fork"/" from conception to consumption" (Article 3);

4.   FBOs carrying out primary production and associated operations must comply with the general requirements of Annex I (Article 4 (1)) and any specific rules in Regulation 853;

5.   FBOs carrying out any stage of production, processing and distribution of food after primary production and associated operations must comply with the general requirements of Annex II (Article 4 (2)) and any specific rules in Regulation 853;

6.   As appropriate, FBOs must adopt specific hygiene measures (Article 4 (3));

       a)   Compliance with microbiological criteria for foodstuffs (see above - Regulation 2073/2005),

       b)   Procedures necessary to meet targets set to achieve the objectives of this Regulation,

       c)   Compliance with temperature control for foodstuffs (e.g. cooking and reheating),

       d)   Maintenance of the cold chain, and

       e)   Sampling and analysis

7.   FBOs must put in place, implement and maintain a permanent procedure or procedures based on the HACCP principles (Article 5);

8.   FBOs must cooperate with the competent authorities and notify them of each establishment under their control or, where required, obtain approval for the food business (Article 6)

The following is a selection of some of the main points arising in practice from the provisions of Regulation 852.

Chapter I – General provisions (Articles 1 and 2)

Regulation 852 does not generally apply to:

1.   Food prepared for private domestic consumption (Article 1 (2) (a) and (b)); and

2.   To the direct supply, by the producer, of small quantities of primary products to the final consumer or to local retail establishments directly supplying the final consumer (Article 1 (2) (c)). This is not defined in Regulation 852 and it is left to Member States to establish rules which "achieve the objectives of this Regulation" (Article 1 (3)).

Food hygiene, hereinafter called 'hygiene', means the measures and conditions necessary to control hazards and to ensure fitness for human consumption of a foodstuff taking into account its intended use (Article 2 (a)).

Chapter II – Food business operators' obligations (Articles 3-6)

Although some of the main points from these Articles have already been mentioned, it may be useful to expand on the requirements to operate a food safety management system (see HACCP – Article 5).

The food safety management system must be business-specific. What might be a suitable system for a large retailer may not be the same for a small bakery, and an "off the shelf" generic food safety management system is unlikely to meet the FBO's needs or satisfy the competent authority.

The system need not be over complicated and, as it has to be under-stood and implemented by staff within the business, there is an argument for saying the simpler the better! A flow chart of key stages and actions is often a useful way of presenting the system.

Some FBOs may decide that they do not need to engage a food safety consultant to assist in creating a food safety management system to protect their customers and their business.

Plenty of guidance on setting up and maintaining a food safety man-agement system is readily available and some competent authorities offer free training to FBOs. This is a very useful resource which if not utilised may be relevant when an FBO is being sentenced for a food offence (see chapter 9).

The following general points about the food safety management system/HACCP may be made here:

1. Lead from the top. An obvious point but unless the FBO and senior staff show commitment to achieve good, or best, practice it can be difficult to implement consistently high standards at every level of the organisation. The FBO must understand that they are operating a *food* business not just any old business;

2. Money alone will not create and operate a thriving, robust and suitable system;

3. Make sure the organisation is following the basic procedures of good hygiene such as cleaning, personal hygiene, training, pest control, operating in suitable premises and using suitable equipment, and zoning to prevent cross-contamination;

4. Inform staff about HACCP, explain what it means, why it is important, the consequences of things going wrong and how each member of staff plays an important role in the process. As with all procedures, HACCP will not and cannot work unless man-

agement provides adequate support, not just financial, and staff feel valued and they "buy in" to its ethos;

5. Create a HACCP team. The size of the organisation and the type of activities undertaken will determine the composition of the team but one or more committed staff members must "take ownership" of the HACCP system;

6. Review each stage of the FBO's activities and identify the hazards to see what could go wrong – intake of goods at the wrong temperature, incorrect handling or storage of products, cooking and cooling, display of foods in a serve over counter or a fridge at the wrong temperature;

7. Critical Control Point (CCP) – how to control the hazards. An obvious one might be to cook food at the right temperature for the correct length of time;

8. Critical limits – to check that the CCP is working by specifying the actual temperature and length of time of the cooking process that will kill pathogens such as *E.coli* O157;

9. Monitor how the CCP is being controlled and record events such as cooking or the temperature of a food in a refrigerator or hot holding facility;

10. Corrective actions to be taken when the monitoring process indicates that a CCP is not under control. If a product has been outside the "safe" temperature for a period of time, what should happen to the product? Can it be used safely or should it be discarded?

11. Verify the system in action to check it is working effectively and if not make changes, record them and retrain staff as appropriate;

12. Suitable documentation and records must be maintained, kept up to date and checked by supervisors. If they indicate a potential

problem this should be investigated. Supervisors should also make random checks of the matters being recorded (i.e. actually check the temperature of the food and not just record the temperature of the equipment or storage unit). Don't always rely on what is written on the document; it may not be accurate.

<u>The Annexes</u>

Although the legislation tells FBOs what to achieve it leaves them to find the most suitable way of achieving this within their own business.

This can be seen in the use of words such as "where necessary"; "where appropriate"; "adequate" and "sufficient" which are interpreted in a way that achieves the objectives of the Regulation (Article 2 (3)).

The Annexes set out the rules applicable to FBOs involved in primary production and associated operations in relation to animals, plants, fish and game (Annex I) and FBOs involved at stages after primary production (Annex II).

Annex I includes requirements to protect food from contamination, keep facilities clean, for training staff on health risks, cleanliness of animals going to slaughter and record-keeping.

Annex II covers a number of specific topics including the cleanliness and structure of the premises, marquees, market stalls, vans, transporting food, keeping articles and equipment which come into contact with food clean and disinfected, handling food waste, personal hygiene and staff illness, protecting foods from contamination, controlling pests and training.

By way of example, reference may be made to the following.

Annex II, Chapter I, paragraph 4 states:

> *"An adequate number of washbasins is to be available, suitably located and designated for cleaning hands. Washbasins for*

> *cleaning hands are to be provided with hot and cold running water, materials for cleaning hands and for hygienic drying. Where necessary, the facilities for washing food are to be separate from the hand-washing facility."*

This provision was the subject of a reference for a preliminary ruling to the Court of Justice of the European Union under Article 267 of the TFEU by the Austrian Courts in a case concerning a public house which served "almost no food, except toast". The washing facility in the premises was equipped with hot running water which could be used for washing hands but was also used for washing dishes.

The Court of Justice made the following remarks:

1.   A wash basin for the purposes of paragraph 4 does not mean one that must be used exclusively for washing hands;

2.   The final sentence of paragraph 4 makes clear that the same basin may be used for washing hands and for washing food, otherwise there would be no need to require that, where necessary, hands and food must be washed in separate equipment;

3.   As the phrase "where necessary" must be read having regard to the objectives of the rules, it is not necessary to have a washing facility exclusively for washing hands where there is a facility for washing food (it all depends on the circumstances, the hazards and the risks and what steps are needed to protect consumers).

See *Astrid Preissl KEG v Landeshauptmann von Wien* (Case C-381/10).

Another case heard by the Court of Justice is also instructive as to the approach to interpreting and applying the food hygiene legislation.

In *Albrecht and others v Landeshauptmann von Wien* (Case C- 382/10).

The applicable provision in that case was Annex II, Chapter IX, paragraph 3;

"At all stages of production, processing and distribution, food is to be protected against any contamination likely to render the food unfit for human consumption, injurious to health or contaminated in such a way that it would be unreasonable to expect it to be consumed in that state."

1. The Austrian authorities directed traders to install containers for the self-service supply of bread and bakery products so they could only be removed using technical means such as tongs, and once items had been removed they could not be replaced;

2. The risk identified by the authorities was that the containers, which were already in use in Germany without undue cause for concern, allowed customers to touch and remove the products by hand, or cough or sneeze on them and could replace product which they had already removed. These activities could cause germs to be deposited on the products;

3. The authorities did not present evidence of actual contamination of the products;

4. Experts in Germany and Austria opined that the use of the containers did not create hygiene problems and as such it was reasonable for the traders to have regard to this when selecting the containers for use;

5. In all the circumstances the Court stated that:

    • it cannot be concluded that food business operators have infringed paragraph 3 on the basis only of the finding that a potential purchaser could conceivably have touched the foodstuffs by hand or sneezed on them;

    • it was necessary to consider the food safety management system implemented by the traders under Article 5 (to prevent, eliminate or reduce to acceptable levels the hazards); and

- the authorities must determine that the food safety management system was insufficient in the light of all the available relevant information.

The mere presence of a risk that someone might sneeze on the bread, which might cause contamination, and might replace the bread was, on the facts of the case, insufficient to show a breach of chapter IX, paragraph 3.

Hygiene of foodstuffs – laying down specific hygiene rules for food of animal origin Regulation 853/2004

Article 1 (1) of Regulation 853/2004 states that the Regulation, "lays down specific rules on the hygiene of food of animal origin for food business operators. These rules supplement those laid down by Regulation 852/2004. They shall apply to unprocessed and processed products of animal origin."

General non-application of Regulation 853

Regulation 853 does not apply to:

a) primary production for private domestic use;

b) the domestic preparation, handling or storage of food for private domestic consumption;

c) the direct supply, by the producer, of small quantities of primary products to the final consumer or to local retail establishments directly supplying the final consumer;

d) the direct supply, by the producer, of small quantities of meat from poultry and lagomorphs slaughtered on the farm to the final consumer or to local retail establishments directly supplying such meat to the final consumer as fresh meat;

e)   hunters who supply small quantities of wild game or wild game meat directly to the final consumer or to local retail establishments directly supplying the final consumer; and

f)   retail (although there are particular rules applying to retail that must be examined on a case by case basis – see for example Article 1(5))

Rules governing the activities referred to in paragraphs (c), (d) and (e) are set by each Member State (Article 1 (4)).

For example, the Food Standards Agency provides guidance in the Food Law Practice Guidance (November 2017 – at pages 23-31). Compliance with those provisions allows farmers to sell some primary products direct to the final consumer "over the farm gate" or at farmer's markets. They would also be able to sell some products to local retailers and restaurants where those establishments directly supply the final consumer.

Consumers may be directly supplied in person (delivery or collection) or remotely (mail order or internet sales) and they need not be "local" to the producer.

Definitions for the purposes of Regulation 853

For the purposes of applying Regulation 853, Annex I contains important definitions including; meat, live bivalve molluscs, fishery products, milk, eggs, frogs' legs and snails.

'Products of animal origin' means: food of animal origin, including honey and blood; live bivalve molluscs, live echinoderms, live tunicates and live marine gastropods intended for human consumption; and other animals destined to be prepared with a view to being supplied live to the final consumer.

Under the heading "meat" in Annex I, are definitions of "mechanically separated meat" (paragraph 1.14) and "meat preparations" (paragraph

1.15). These seemingly innocuous terms have been the subject of a long series of cases before the English Courts and upon a preliminary reference to the Court of Justice of the European Union and readers may find the discussion and debate of interest particularly regarding the Courts' approaches to legislative interpretation and the scope of an English court which does not wish to blindly apply an interpretation given by the CJEU.

The challenge arose in proceedings for judicial review of a decision made by the Food Standards Agency (FSA) to classify Newby Foods' product as "mechanically separated meat" (MSM). The initial reported case is under the heading of *R (on the application of Newby Foods Ltd) v Food Standards Agency* [2013] EWHC 1966 (Admin). At the time of writing (early 2018) an appeal to the Supreme Court is pending.

Some other aspects of Regulation 853

Premises/establishments

Only products prepared and handled exclusively in establishments that meet the applicable requirements of food law and have been registered or, where required, approved by the competent authority may be placed on the market (Article 4).

With certain exceptions, establishments handling products of animal origin for which Annex III to Regulation 853 lays down specific requirements (e.g. transporting and slaughtering animals) require approval by the relevant competent authority before they can operate.

Annex III covers products of animal origin including: meat from various animals (cattle, pigs, poultry, lagomorphs and game); minced meat, meat preparations, meat products and mechanically separated meat; fish, milk, eggs and frogs' legs and snails. It sets out, in many respects quite detailed, requirements covering many aspects of production of these products such as the layout of premises), hygiene matters, compositional requirements and labelling.

Product marking

Product of animal origin may only be placed on the market if it has been handled in an establishment subject to approval and it has either:

(a) a health mark applied in accordance with Regulation (EC) No 854/2004;

or

(b) when that Regulation does not provide for the application of a health mark, an identification mark applied in accordance with Annex II, Section I, of this Regulation

The mark is commonly seen as an oval logo containing a country code, UK or IE, and the approval number of the establishment.

It should be noted that there are additional specific labelling requirements for other products such as beef.

Practical application – enforcement action under the hygiene regulations

Enforcement action for non-compliance with the hygiene rules might result in the service of an enforcement notice and/or a criminal prosecution.

The FBO's response to either or both of these events depends on a careful assessment of the situation; is the enforcement officer's assessment of the circumstances accepted; what is the impact of the action on the food business; can steps be taken to minimise the impact of the action (e.g. conduct a deep clean and re-open the business within a day or two); what are the cost and other resource implications of compliance and/or challenging the action.

It is very important that the official's factual assessment of the conditions in the food business is assessed in light of the purpose and objective of food hygiene legislation.

It might be very difficult to argue that a photograph showing raw meat placed directly above ready to eat salad with the consequential dripping of meat juice onto the salad is anything other than a contravention. There may be actual contamination or at least the realistic potential for contamination (see for example Regulation 852, Annex II, Chapter IX, paragraph 3)

However, cracked floor tiles in a restaurant may not be capable of being effectively cleaned and should be placed or repaired but, depending on the circumstances, the effect of this defect *may* not be sufficient to amount to a breach requiring enforcement action, having regard to the purpose and objective of the legislation (see for example Regulation 852 Annex II, Chapter 1, paragraph 1).

There may be a difference between action that *should* be taken to make good minor deficiencies as a matter of good practice and those steps which *must* be taken to remedy a legal contravention. The two can become blurred and competent authorities must ensure the distinction is maintained, particularly in an inspection report requiring the FBO to take corrective action.

All circumstances are different and each situation must be looked individually having regard, as appropriate, to first principles including the identification of a hazard and then assessing the risk consequential on that hazard.

CHAPTER FOUR
LABELLING AND FOOD INFORMATION TO CONSUMERS

Introduction

Providing consumers with sufficient information to allow them to make informed choices about the food they consume is one of the main pillars of food law.

This information may be provided on the product label, on a restaurant menu, on a website or in other advertising or marketing material.

These information rules may be divided into general requirements contained in Regulation (EU) No 1169/2011 on the provision of food information to consumers (in this chapter referred to as EUFIC) and those additional rules specific to a food or food type (e.g. chocolate or food supplements).

This information may be required to keep consumers safe (warning them about substances causing allergies – peanuts for example) or to allow them to make personal choices (following a vegetarian or vegan diet).

Food business operators (FBOs) may make statements or claims about their products which are not included in legislation for example, "natural", "pure" or "fresh". When advising on compliance it may be necessary to have regard to guidance issued by the competent authorities and others.

Advising a food business operator (FBO) on labelling and food information requirements often involves a consideration of different pieces of legislation and guidance and may require reference to case law and decisions of regulators such as the Advertising Standards Authority and others.

It may be necessary to correctly categorise the food to establish which specific rules apply and thereafter to see whether other legislation is relevant (e.g. nutrition and health claims – see chapter 5).

The provision of information is also subject to developments in food policy which may affect the food itself (e.g. compositional changes to reduce salt, sugar, fat etc.) or the way in which information is provided (e.g. traffic lights to denote levels of salt, sugar, fat etc.).

There are so many rules and requirements that touch on food information and labelling that it is impossible to include them all. This chapter will therefore review the main provisions of EUFIC and refer briefly to some other labelling rules.

The Provision of Food Information to Consumers Regulation 1169/2011 (EUFIC)

References to Articles in the parts of this chapter relate to EUFIC unless specifically stated to be otherwise.

Although this is an EU Regulation and directly applicable in each Member State, there are some national differences and, as always, local market advice should be taken.

EUFIC replaced the previous rules relating to general food labelling (Directive 2000/13/EC) and the provision of nutrition information (Directive 90/496/EEC). The main provisions of the legislation took effect on 13th December 2014 and the requirement for a mandatory nutrition declaration came into force on 13th December 2016.

Although EUFIC provides detailed requirements for the provision of food information, it has been the subject of various guidance documents, EU reports and legislation which have expanded or clarified the main rules, particularly around providing country of origin information. These often provide useful assistance on the practical application of the legislation.

Any food intended for supply to the final consumer or to mass caterers must be accompanied by food information in accordance with EUFIC (Article 6).

Food information is broadly defined as: "information concerning a food and made available to the final consumer by means of a label, other accompanying material, or any other means including modern technology tools or verbal communication" (Article 2(2)).

Article 2 contains definitions including:

Mandatory food information

The particulars that are required to be provided to the final consumer by Union provisions.

Prepacked food

Any single item for presentation as such to the final consumer and to mass caterers, consisting of a food and the packaging into which it was put before being offered for sale, whether such packaging encloses the food completely or only partially, but in any event in such a way that the contents cannot be altered without opening or changing the packaging.

Mass caterer

Any establishment (including a vehicle or a fixed or mobile stall), such as restaurants, canteens, schools, hospitals and catering enterprises in which, in the course of a business, food is prepared to be ready for consumption by the final consumer.

Ingredient

Any substance or product, including flavourings, food additives and food enzymes, and any constituent of a compound ingredient, used in the manufacture or preparation of a food and still present in the finished product, even if in an altered form; residues shall not be considered as 'ingredients'

Labelling

Any words, particulars, trademarks, brand name, pictorial matter or symbol relating to a food and placed on any packaging, document, notice, label, ring or collar accompanying or referring to such food.

Article 3 (2) gives effect to the principle of free movement of "legally produced and marketed food", taking into account "the need to protect the legitimate interests of producers".

Article 7 sets out some general principles under the heading of "Fair Information Practices" and provides that food information:

- must not be misleading;

- must be accurate, clear and easy to understand for the consumer;

- must not attribute the property of preventing, treating or curing a human disease, nor refer to such properties

Those prohibitions also apply to advertising and to the general way in which foods are presented (e.g. shape, appearance or packaging).

Article 44 of EUFIC concerns the rules applicable to "non-prepacked food" and provides for rules to be set at national level, "where foods are offered for sale to the final consumer or to mass caterers without pre-packaging, or where foods are packed on the sales premises at the consumer's request or prepacked for direct sale".

This is not always as straightforward as it may seem and reference should be made to local market rules and guidance.

Responsibilities for food information – Article 8

Article 8 sets out detailed provisions for establishing who is responsible for providing food information along the food chain.

As may be expected, primary responsibility for ensuring the presence and accuracy of food information rests with the FBO under whose name the food is marketed. If that FBO is established outside the European Union then the importer is responsible.

Some FBOs, such as retailers, simply buy and sell foodstuffs without doing anything to affect the food information. FBOs are deemed to know the rules and must not supply foods which they know or presume, on the basis of information in their possession, to be non-compliant.

Within their businesses, FBOs must not modify food information if this would mislead the final consumer, reduce the level of consumer protection or impede the making of consumer choices. This might apply to extending 'use-by' dates on bulk product (e.g. ham) that the FBO retailer opens and cuts up for sale to consumers (e.g. for sandwiches).

Each FBO must provide proper food information to the next FBO in line so when food is supplied to the final consumer it is properly labelled (maintaining the integrity of the "information chain").

A break in the information chain could create a safety issue for consumers with allergies and could significantly mislead consumers including vegetarians and vegans who have chosen only to eat certain types of foods.

Mandatory food information – Article 9 and 10

Articles 9 and 10 of EUFIC set out the mandatory food information (MFI) required in prepacked food.

The mandatory particulars as set out in Article 9 (1):

(a) the name of the food;

(b) the list of ingredients;

(c) any ingredient or processing aid listed in Annex II or derived from a substance or product listed in Annex II causing allergies or intolerances used in the manufacture or preparation of a food and still present in the finished product, even if in an altered form;

(d) the quantity of certain ingredients or categories of ingredients (QUID);

(e) the net quantity of the food;

(f) the date of minimum durability or the 'use by' date;

(g) any special storage conditions and/or conditions of use;

(h) the name or business name and address of the food business operator referred to in Article 8(1);

(i) the country of origin or place of provenance where provided for in Article 26;

(j) instructions for use where it would be difficult to make appro-priate use of the food in the absence of such instructions;

(k) with respect to beverages containing more than 1,2 % by volume of alcohol, the actual alcoholic strength by volume;

(l)   a nutrition declaration.

Although Article 9 contains a list of mandatory food information, it is supplemented by detailed rules in other parts of EUFIC (e.g. Articles 12 – 35 and associated Annexes) and a number of guidance documents at EU and national level.

Ingredients causing allergies or intolerances (Article 9 (1) (c))

Substances causing allergies or intolerances are relevant to four main topics:

1)   Hygiene law – preventing inadvertent cross-contamination;

2)   General food law – placing unsafe food on the market;

3)   General criminal law – prosecutions, including the offence of manslaughter (see *R v Mohammed Khalique Zaman* [2017] EWCA Crim 1783 by way of example); and

4)   Food information law – warning consumers about the presence of those substances which are actually used in the manufacture or production of the food and which are still present in the final product.

There are 14 "substances or products causing allergies or intolerances" set out in Annex II to EUFIC. Food information law only applies to these 14 substances or products even though some people may have reactions to other foodstuffs (for example strawberries or kiwi fruit).

The 14 are:

1. Cereals containing gluten, namely: wheat (such as spelt and khorasan wheat), rye, barley, oats or their hybridised strains, and products thereof;

2. Crustaceans and products thereof;

3. Eggs and products thereof;

4. Fish and products thereof;

5. Peanuts and products thereof;

6. Soybeans and products thereof:

7. Milk and products thereof (including lactose);

8. Nuts, namely: almonds (Amygdalus communis L.), hazelnuts (Corylus avellana), walnuts (Juglans regia), cashews (Anacardium occidentale), pecan nuts (Carya illinoinensis (Wangenh.) K. Koch), Brazil nuts (Bertholletia excelsa), pistachio nuts (Pistacia vera), macadamia or Queensland nuts (Macadamia ternifolia), and products thereof, except for nuts used for making alcoholic distillates including ethyl alcohol of agricultural origin;

9. Celery and products thereof;

10. Mustard and products thereof;

11. Sesame seeds and products thereof;

12. Sulphur dioxide and sulphites at concentrations of more than 10 mg/kg or 10 mg/litre in terms of the total SO2 which are to be calculated for products as proposed ready for consumption or as reconstituted according to the instructions of the manufacturers;

13. Lupin and products thereof;

14.   Molluscs and products thereof.

Allergens - prepacked foods – Article 21

Any of the above ingredients present in the final food must be listed within the list of ingredients "with a clear reference to the name of the substance or product" which must be "emphasised through a typeset that clearly distinguishes it from the rest of the list of ingredients, for example by means of the font, style or background colour."

This is usually indicated by a statement on the label adjacent to the list of ingredients, "for allergens see ingredients in ..." followed by in bold, red or however the FBO has chosen to highlight the ingredient.

When developing the label, it is important to see how this actually looks in practice to ensure that the particular substance "stands out from the other ingredients". The quality of the printing, typeset and clarity of colours on the final label may have an impact on this.

Where the food does not require a list of ingredients (see Article 19) the information is provided by using the word "contains" followed by the correct name of the allergenic ingredient; for example, a wine label would state; "Contains – Sulphites".

Allergens - non-prepacked foods – Article 44

Article 44 of EUFIC states that all allergenic ingredients must be provided along with any other mandatory food information prescribed by a Member State.

This has been applied differently throughout the EU and reference must be made to local market rules. It is becoming common to see a menu in a restaurant refer to these ingredients by putting a number next to the particular food or dish with a note setting out a numbered list of the "allergen" ingredients. Sometimes the information is provided in a table or matrix which contains all the foodstuffs with an indication of which of the 14 ingredients applies to each food/product.

The FBO must positively take appropriate steps to provide the necessary allergen information to consumers or tell them where they find that information (in compliance with national rules). It is not sufficient for the FBO to simply rely on the consumer raising the issue of allergens.

Precautionary statements – "may contain" – risk of inadvertent cross-contamination

Although one or more of the 14 substances may not have been used as an ingredient in a foodstuff it may have been made in premises that handle one or more of them. If there is a real chance that the final product might inadvertently contain one or more of the 14 due to inadvertent cross-contamination, the label or information can say "may contain" followed by the name of the ingredient. This should only be done following a proper risk assessment rather than simply as means of protecting the FBO.

Awareness of problems with allergens

Providing allergen information can be challenging, particularly in sectors such as hospitality, and requires all staff to be fully trained in relation to the 14 substances and how these are used in the final food. Great care must be taken to update the allergen information when introducing new foods to the menu, developing existing recipes or changing suppliers.

Due to the serious implications of susceptible consumers eating food which contains these substances, some FBOs are training staff in how to identify and respond to consumers who have adverse reactions.

Date of minimum durability and use by date (Article 9 (1) (f))

A "date of minimum durability" (a best before date) is an indication of the timeframe within which the food retains its optimum qualities. Beyond this date food will deteriorate and may not taste as "fresh" but may still be safe to eat.

This date is replaced by a "use by" date where from, a microbiological point of view, foods are highly perishable and are therefore likely after a short period to constitute an immediate danger to human health" (Article 24).

As the use by date concerns safety, food should not be consumed once the use by date has expired. This is highly relevant to general food law issues in that Article 24 states, "after the 'use by' date a food shall be deemed to be unsafe in accordance with Article 14(2) to (5) of Regulation (EC) No 178/2002".

This imposes stringent obligations on FBOs to have a clear, robust and functioning system around stock rotation.

Mandatory nutrition information – Article 9 (1) (l)

Section 3 of EUFIC provides detailed information about how this information is provided. This does not apply to food supplements and natural mineral waters which are governed by their own rules (Article 29).

When reading the provisions of EUFIC for the first time, or even on subsequent occasions, the rules can seem rather complex and confusing. A number of organisations, including many of the competent authorities, have produced useful guidance on this subject.

Although reference must always be had to the legislation (EU and at national level) these guides can very helpful to get the overall picture about what is required and how it should be presented.

The following is therefore a note of some, but not all, of the general requirements relating to mandatory nutrition information (see Annex V for foods that are exempt from this requirement).

The mandatory nutrition declaration *must* include (Article 30 (1)) – often referred to as "back of pack":

> *The energy value;*
>
> *And the amounts of -*
>
> *fat; saturates; carbohydrate; sugars; protein and salt*

The FBO may choose to repeat that information and this is often referred to as "front of pack" information (Article 30 (3)). The FBO may only repeat information by stating:

> *The energy value, or*
>
> *The energy value together with the amounts of fat, saturates, sugars and salt.*

Article 30 (2) states that the mandatory nutrition declaration *may* be supplemented by providing the amounts of one or more of:

> *Mono-unsaturates; Polyunsaturates; Polyols; Starch; Fibre; any of the vitamins or minerals in compliance with the rules in Annex XIII of EUFIC (including vitamins such as A and C and minerals such as calcium and potassium).*

The rules provide for how this information is to be provided.

Other aspects of the rules concern: non-prepacked food (Articles 30 (5) and 44); how to calculate the values for the ingredients (Articles 30 (1), 30 (5) and 31 (3)) and how to display information (e.g. per 100 g/100 ml and per portion – Articles 32 and 33) and the method of presentation (Article 34).

As well as FBOs checking the accuracy of their information, competent authorities may take samples to check composition levels against the values stated on pack. It is therefore important that the FBO can readily and easily substantiate and support the amounts declared on pack and provide that information to the authority if required.

Additional mandatory particulars – Article 10 and Annex III

Mandatory information, the precise details of which are prescribed, must be given for the following:

- Foods packaged in certain gases to extend their durability;

- Foods containing sweeteners;

- Foods containing glycyrrhizinic acid (liquorice);

- Beverages with high caffeine content and foods with added caffeine;

- Foods with added phytosterols, phytosterol esters, phytostanols or phytostanol esters; and

- Frozen meat, frozen meat preparations and frozen unprocessed fishery products

Presentation of mandatory food information

Articles 12 and 13 prescribe how mandatory information is to be presented:

- It must be available and easily accessible for all foods;

- For prepacked foods it must appear directly on the package or on a label attached thereto;

- It must be marked in a conspicuous place in such a way as to be easily visible, clearly legible and, where appropriate, indelible. It must not in any way be hidden, obscured, detracted from or interrupted by any other written or pictorial matter or any other intervening material;

- It must be of the appropriate font size (1.2 mm or 0.9 mm)

- The name of the food, the net quantity and, where appropriate, the actual alcoholic strength by volume must appear in the same field of vision

Article 14 sets out rules applying to foods (prepacked and non-prepacked) "offered by means of distance communication" including via the internet.

Article 15 states that mandatory food information must be "in a language easily understood by the consumers of the Member States where a food is marketed". Member States may prescribe what those languages are to be and this may be more than one language (e.g. in Ireland – English or English and Irish). This is important when advising clients seeking to sell goods in new markets.

It is also important because if certain information, for example substances causing allergens, is not provided in the "correct" language for the market this may require a product recall.

Omission of certain mandatory particulars – Article 16

Article 16 provides a list of products which do not require full mandatory particulars. These include certain glass bottles, small packages (largest surface having an area of less than 10 cm2); products containing more than 1.2% alcohol).

Voluntary food information – Articles 36 and 37

Where mandatory food information as referred to in Articles 9 and 10 is provided on a voluntary basis, it must comply with applicable provisions of EUFIC (Article 36).

Voluntary food information must not be misleading, ambiguous or confusing for consumers and it must be based on the relevant scientific data, where this is applicable (Article 36).

Voluntary food information shall not be displayed to the detriment of the space available for mandatory food information (Article 37).

Other labelling issues

This part addresses the product-specific requirements of some foodstuffs in addition to, or instead of, some parts of EUFIC.

The interaction between various labelling rules – the example of food supplements

In addition to EUFIC, reference must be had to Directive 2002/46/EC on the law relating to food supplements.

This provides that food supplements:

- Must only be supplied to consumers in a "pre-packaged form" (Article 1);

- Supplement the normal diet by providing "concentrated sources of nutrients or other substances with a nutritional or physiological effect" (Article 2);

- Are marketed in dose form such as "capsules, pastilles, tablets, pills and other similar forms, sachets of powder, ampoules of liquids, drop dispensing bottles, and other similar forms of liquids and powders designed to be taken in measured small unit quantities" (Article 2);

- Have their own labelling rules in addition to, or instead of, EUFIC – for example, food supplements have their own nutrition labelling provisions;

- Are targeted at particular parts of the body (e.g. eyes, heart, bones, hair, skin);

- May include health claims on their labels (e.g. Thiamine; "contributes to the normal function of the heart" – see next chapter);

- May be required to contain voluntary warning or advisory statements where the product contains certain substances (e.g. certain such vitamins and minerals at particular levels);

Having regard to the above there is a risk that the marketing or labelling of a food supplement might get close to stating or implying that the product will cure or treat a disease or bodily condition.

If so, the product may cease to be a food and become a medicinal product by presentation. Article 1 (2) of Directive 2001/83/EC on medicinal products defines a medicinal product, by presentation, as; "any substance or combination of substances presented as having properties for treating or preventing disease in human beings" and is to be interpreted broadly.

Article 2 of Directive 2001/83/EC states; "in cases of doubt, where, taking into account all its characteristics, a product may fall within the definition of a 'medicinal product' and within the definition of a product covered by other Community legislation the provisions of this Directive shall apply".

If a food makes medicinal claims it becomes regulated by the, harsher, medicinal products regime but it may also breach Article 7 (3) of EUFIC relating to fair information practices; "food information shall not attribute to any food the property of preventing, treating or curing a human disease, nor refer to such properties".

Crossing the line form a food to a medicinal product can have very serious consequences for the FBO, its business and its products.

Foods for specific groups

This is one of the food groups that are regulated differently from "ordinary" foods.

Regulation (EU) No 609/2013 on Foods for Specific Groups (FSG) replaced PARNUTS law (foods for particular nutritional purposes) from 20th July 2016 and covers:

• Infant and follow on formula;

• Processed cereal based food/baby food;

• Food for special medical purposes;

• Total diet replacement for weight control

Earlier in the book reference was made to the principle of mutual recognition (free movement of goods within the EU). Article 4 (3) of the FSG Regulation states: "Member States may not restrict or forbid the placing on the market of food which complies with this Regulation, for reasons related to its composition, manufacture, presentation or labelling".

Young-child formulae and food intended for sportspeople which were subject to PARNUTS rules are not covered by FSG and are now subject to general food laws.

Even within the FSG Regulation itself, some foods are subject to strict product-specific rules about how they are presented to consumers. Article 10 of the FSG Regulation concerns the labelling, presentation and advertising of infant formula and follow-on formula which must not discourage breast-feeding and which must not include, "pictures of infants, or other pictures or text which may idealise the use of such formulae".

This may be seen as an interaction between labelling law, nutrition and health and social policy and is a global topic of interest.

Finally, the overarching provisions of the FSG Regulation are supplemented by various Delegated EU legislation to which reference must be made.

Food Improvement Agents

Food Improvement Agents are:

- *Enzymes having biochemical actions which can be used in food production by breaking down the structure of fruit to extract more juice or to convert starch into sugar in alcohol production* (Regulation (EC) No 1332/2008);

- *Additives used for preserving, colouring and stabilising food (among many other uses)* (Regulation (EC) No 1333/2008); and

- *Flavourings to change colour or taste of food* (Regulation (EC) No 1334/2008)

These substances are subject to a common authorisation procedure contained in Regulation (EC) No 1331/2008 and the Regulations are supplemented by a series of implementing provisions and are subject to regular revisions and updates.

Food Improvement Agents are very common in food production, although their use must be approved in accordance with the applicable legislation, which might restrict or prohibit the use of FIAs in certain types of food.

The legislation prescribes how FIAs are to be labelled when used as ingredients in food sold to consumers and when they are not intended for sale to the final consumer.

By way of example the list of ingredients on a food label might include reference to the sweetener, E 960 Steviol Glycosides. The 'E' number, and category of FIA (preservative, sweetener, colour etc.) can be found in Annex II of Regulation 1333/2008.

There is a particular labelling requirement in respect of foods containing the so-called "Southampton" colours listed in Annex V of the Additives Regulation; Sunset yellow (E 110), Quinoline yellow (E 104), Carmoisine (E 122), Allura red (E 129), Tartrazine (E 102) and Ponceau 4R (E 124)

Where those colours are present in food, Article 24 and Annex V of Regulation 1333/2008 provide that the labelling must contain the statement after naming the colour; "may have an adverse effect on activity and attention in children".

Practical Application

Correctly classifying the food is crucial because without that inform-ation the FBO and their advisers do not know which regulatory scheme applies.

This point was highlighted above in connection with food supplements and medicinal products, but the point can be seen from the case of The Queen on the application of Nutricia Limited and The Secretary of State for Health [2015] EWHC 2285 (Admin), concerning whether or not a product could be "classified as a food for special medical purposes or "FSMP"".

At paragraph 22 of his judgment, Green J said:

> *"Under both EU and domestic law products intended to provide some form of nutritional supplementation to the human diet fall into four broad categories: fortified foods; food supplements; foods for particular nutritional uses (known as "PARNUTs"); and foods for special medical purposes ("FSMPs"). Each category is subject to a distinct regulatory framework."*

Information is conveyed to consumers by means of all the information on a product label and hence the use of words in a particular context may be important in establishing legal compliance.

The case of *Bundesverband der Verbraucherzentralen und Verbraucher-verbände – Verbraucherzentrale Bundesverband eV v Teekanne GmbH and Co KG* (C-195/14) might be instructive to how these issues arise. The question arose as to whether or not a food label was misleading. Although the case was based on the previous general labelling regime contained in Directive 2000/13/EC, the general principles apply equally to EUFIC.

A food label contained images of raspberries and vanilla flowers and therefore a consumer might, perhaps reasonably, believe that they were contained in the product. The list of ingredients did not include references to these substances and hence, by omission, advised consumers that the product did not, in fact, contain them.

As consumers are expected to have regard to all the available information, the question arose as to whether the label was misleading in that the clear visual implication that the product contained raspberries and/or vanilla was only dispelled once the consumer carefully read the list of ingredients.

In its decision on a reference for a preliminary ruling from the German courts, the Court of Justice of the European Union advised that an accurate and complete list of ingredients might not be sufficient to correct the erroneous or misleading impression which the consumer gains from the labelling of the foodstuff.

Where the labelling of a foodstuff gives the impression that a particular ingredient is present in that foodstuff, even though it is not in fact present (this being apparent solely from the list of ingredients), the label could mislead the purchaser as to the characteristics of the foodstuff in question.

Whether the label is misleading is a question of fact and law for the national courts to determine.

Due to the complex nature of food information and food labelling it is not always possible to provide definitive advice on the legality of a label or related marketing material having regard to food law. It is often possible to say that a phrase is not permissible, a red flag, (e.g. stating a food supplement will cure arthritis) or it is permissible, a green flag, (e.g. strictly following the legal requirement for example regarding the presentation of the mandatory nutrition declaration, or correctly using a nutrition or health claim – see chapter 5).

Sometimes the advice might require an orange, or amber, flag. The phrase or statement may be on the "cusp of compliance" and becoming compliant may require a, perhaps subtle, change of wording or emphasis or context, or it might depend on how others (competent authorities, consumers and commercial competitors) interpret the information conveyed.

Ultimately, where a label is challenged, and the parties cannot reach agreement on the application of the relevant rules, only a court can provide a definitive interpretation of the law in any given set of circumstances. Neither party may want matters to go that far.

Conclusion

Advising on labelling and food information is not always straightforward; there are many different rules to be taken into account.

Additionally, the adviser may need to be aware of potential "tensions", or competing interests, between the needs, requirements and desires of the FBO, the legal and compliance team and those involved in marketing and advertising. This may require a degree of compromise when finalising the information that will appear on the label.

There is clear scope for creativity and innovation in the development of food labels and other methods of communicating with consumers, but this is dependent on having an understanding of the basic rules and how they may be used legally to the FBO's advantage.

CHAPTER FIVE
NUTRITION AND
HEALTH CLAIMS

Introduction

Food business operators are keen to promote their products in most commercially advantageous way whilst remaining legally compliant.

One way of achieving this may be to emphasise the benefits of a food generally or specifically because of an ingredient that it contains or does not contain.

The making of nutrition and health claims is governed by Regulation (EC) No 1924/2006 on nutrition and health claims made on foods (hereafter in this chapter, the NHCR).

This chapter will review some of the main provision of this legislation.

The Nutrition and Health Claims Regulation – general provisions

The NHCR contains rules governing claims generally and specifically to nutrition claims and to health claims.

As stated in Article 1, the NHCR applies to nutrition and health claims made in "commercial communications, whether in the labelling, presentation or advertising of foods to be delivered as such to the final consumer".

An issue that arises in practice is whether the making of the claim is in a "commercial communication", a term not defined in the NHCR.

Guidance on what is, and what is not a commercial communication can be found in Recital 4 of the NHCR which states that dietary guidelines or advice issued by public health authorities are communications that are not commercial in nature.

Further guidance may be found in a decision of the Court of Justice of the European Union, *Verband Sozialer Wettbewerb* (Case C-19/15) in which the Court had regard to other EU legislation in which the term commercial communication is defined and stated that in the context of the NHCR the term included a communication made in the form of advertising foods, designed to promote, directly or indirectly, those foods (see paragraph 29 of the Judgment).

The following definitions are taken from Article 2 of the NHCR:

Claim

Means any message or representation, which is not mandatory under Community or national legislation, including pictorial, graphic or symbolic representation, in any form, which states, suggests or implies that a food has particular characteristics.

Nutrition claim

Means any claim which states, suggests or implies that a food has particular beneficial nutritional properties due to:

(a)   the energy (calorific value) it

   (i) provides;

   (ii) provides at a reduced or increased rate; or

   (iii) does not provide; and/or

(b)   the nutrients or other substances it

(i) contains;

(ii) contains in reduced or increased proportions; or

(iii) does not contain;

The claim must state, suggest or imply a *benefit* arising from the presence or absence of energy or nutrients.

Health claim

Means any claim that states, suggests or implies that a relationship exists between a food category, a food or one of its constituents and health

Article 2 also states that definitions in other food law legislation apply for the purposes of the NHCR. This includes the basic definitions of "food", "food business operator" and "placing on the market" from Regulation (EC) No 178/2002; the General Food Law Regulation.

Principles for all claims

Article 3 states that the use of nutrition and health claims must not:

a) *Be false, misleading or ambiguous;*

b) *Give rise to doubt about the safety and/or nutritional adequacy of other foods;*

c) *Encourage or condone excess consumption of a food;*

d) *State, suggest or imply that a balanced and varied diet cannot provide appropriate quantities of nutrients in general;*

e) *Refer to changes in bodily functions which could give rise to or exploit fear in the consumer, either textually or through pictorial, graphic or symbolic representations.*

Alcoholic beverages and claims (Article 4)

Beverages containing more than 1.2% by volume of alcohol may not bear health claims.

They may contain the following nutrition claims: referring to low alcohol levels, the reduction of the alcohol content, or the reduction of energy content.

It should be noted that until 13th December 2018, some descriptions applied to alcoholic beverages in the UK, in the Food Labelling Regulations 1996 remain in force. These are "alcohol-free", "dealcoholised", "low alcohol" (and any other word or description which implies that the drink being described is low in alcohol) and "non-alcoholic".

General conditions of use

Article 5 prescribes the general conditions of use for nutrition and health claims which must be based on accepted science, the substance must be present in a significant quantity in the final product and nutrition and health claims shall only be permitted if the average consumer can be expected to understand the beneficial effects as expressed in the claim.

Nutrition and health claims refer to the food ready for consumption in accordance with the manufacturer's instructions.

The FBO must be able to justify any claims they use (see Article 6).

Nutrition claims – specific requirements

Nutrition claims - introduction

A nutrition claim may only be made if it is contained in the Annex to the NHCR and its conditions of use are complied with.

Nutrition claims set out in the Annex to the NHCR include: low energy, low fat; low sodium/salt; high fibre; high protein; high (followed by a reference to a specified vitamin or mineral).

The Annex states that the permitted nutrition claim (e.g. source of fibre) "and any claim likely to have the same meaning for the consumer" must comply with the conditions of use specified in the Annex. Therefore, to say "contains fibre" might have the same meaning as "source of fibre" and can only be used if the conditions of use for "source of fibre" are fulfilled.

Comparative claims (Article 9)

It is permissible to make a comparative nutrition claim between foods of the same category and the Annex contains certain comparative nutrition claims including, 'increased' (followed by the name of the nutrient) where the conditions of use are:

> *"A claim stating that the content in one or more nutrients, other than vitamins and minerals, has been increased, and any claim likely to have the same meaning for the consumer, may only be made where the product meets the conditions for the claim 'source of' and the increase in content is at least 30 % compared to a similar product."*

The products subject of the comparison must be clearly identified to the consumer and although "foods of the same category" is not further defined, the comparator products should be within a group of products that are similar in terms of nutritional content (e.g. cheeses or milks).

Health claims

Health claims - introduction

A health claim may only be used if it is authorised following a positive evaluation by the European Food Safety Authority (EFSA) and included in EU legislation authorising the use of the claim.

Reference may be had to the Annex to Regulation (EU) 432/2012, as amended, and a list of those claims which have been authorised and those which are not authorised may be found in the EU Register of nutrition and health claims made on foods. The Register is very helpful starting point when advising on a potential claim, but regard must always be had to the wording of the particular legislation authorising the wording and use of the claim.

Examples of authorised health claims are; calcium is needed for the maintenance of normal bones, vitamin C contributes to the reduction of tiredness and fatigue and zinc contributes to the maintenance of normal bones.

A health claim relates to the nutrient, substance, food or food category for which they have been authorised and must not be made for the food product that contains them.

For example, it is proposed to use the health claim "thiamine contributes to the normal function of the heart" on a food supplement. Care must be taken to ensure that the claim as made on the label clearly is based on the presence of thiamine and does not relate to the product as a whole. This may be done by listing the authorised health claim immediately followed by the name of the ingredient to which it relates or perhaps by listing the authorised health claim immediately followed by an asterix or another symbol which is then placed next to the ingredient subject to the claim listed elsewhere on the label.

In addition, the conditions of use relating to the quantity of thiamine in the product must also be fulfilled.

It is possible to move away from the actual wording of the authorised health claim, some examples of which are quite scientific and technical, in the interests of better consumer understanding.

However, any changes to the wording must have the same meaning for the consumer as the authorised claim and care must be taken not to enhance or embellish the authorised wording.

Using the above example, "thiamine contributes to the normal function of the heart". Changing the wording to "thiamine makes your heart stronger" or "thiamine will improve the condition of your heart" may be seen as moving too far away from the meaning of the authorised claims and may, depending on context, be seen as making a medicinal claim by reference to curing, healing or preventing heart disease.

As with a lot of labelling and information issues, the words used and the context in which they are used, will be important in assessing compliance.

Once a health claims has been authorised, it may be used by any food business operator as long as the conditions of use are complied with.

Types of health claims

The main types of health claims are:

1.   *Function health claims (Article 13 (1))*

    •   Relating to the growth, development and functions of the body (e.g. calcium is needed for the maintenance of normal teeth;

    •   Referring to psychological and behavioural functions (e.g. magnesium contributes to normal psychological function); and

    •   Slimming or weight-control (e.g. substituting one daily meal of an energy restricted diet with a meal replacement contributes to the maintenance of weight after weight loss)

But note – claims which make reference to the rate or amount of weight loss are not allowed (Article 12 (b))

2.   *Function health claims based on newly developed scientific evidence (Article 13 (5))*

3.   *Risk reduction claims (Article 14 (1) (a)*

   • Reducing a risk factor in the development of a disease (e.g., reduction of blood cholesterol which is a risk factor in the development of coronary heart disease")

4.   *Claims relating to children's development (Article 14 (1) (b)*

   • For example, vitamin D is needed for the normal growth and development of bone in children

5.   *Claims about general or non-specific benefits (Article 10 (3))*

   • For example. "good for you" or "healthy"

   But note – this type of claim may only be made if accompanied by a specific authorised health claim (see Commission Implementing Decision 2013/63/EU for further guidance)

As mentioned above, a health claim is authorised following an evaluation by EFSA. If EFSA provides a positive opinion the matter is then considered by the European Institutions and the Commission prepares a Regulation which states that the proposed claim is either authorised or it is not.

A positive EFSA opinion does not guarantee that the application for authorisation will be successful.

In the case of *Dextro Energy GmbH & Co KG v European Commission* (T-100/15), EFSA had confirmed that claims, relating to glucose, had met the necessary scientific criteria but the Commission had refused to authorise them. The Court of Justice of the European Union ruled in support of the Commission by saying it had not erred in principle in refusing to authorise the claims given that they were incompatible with generally accepted principles of nutrition and health which are to reduce sugar consumption.

Health claim specific conditions

Article 10 of the NHCR imposes specific conditions on the use of health claims and again reference should be made to the exact wording of the provisions.

In terms of labelling, a health claim must be accompanied by the following information, where applicable:

(a) A statement indicating the importance of a varied and balanced diet and a healthy lifestyle;

(b) The quantity of the food and pattern of consumption required to obtain the claimed beneficial effect;

(c) Where appropriate, a statement addressed to persons who should avoid using the food; and

(d) An appropriate warning for products that are likely to present a health risk if consumed to excess

Restrictions on the use of certain health claims – Article 12

The following may not be made:

(a) Claims which suggest that health could be affected by not consuming the food;

(b)   Claims which make reference to the rate or amount of weight loss;

(c)   Claims which make reference to recommendations of individual doctors or health professionals and other associations not referred to in Article 11 (i.e. national associations of medical, nutrition or dietetic professionals and health-related charities).

Point (c) can cause some difficulty in practice. It is possible, with care, for a doctor or health professional to recommend a branded product that is also making a health claim. The relevant issues are to examine the words used, the context in which they are used and how they are positioned on the label or other material.

Conclusion

The NHCR sets out the basic rules governing the use of nutrition and health claims and where these are made reference must be had to the obligations to provide mandatory nutrition information (see chapter 4).

The NHCR refers to the establishment of specific nutrient profiles which food or certain categories of food must comply with in order the bear nutrition or health claims (Article 4). This list was due for completion in January 2009 but at the time of writing, early 2018, the list has not yet been completed.

Finally, the NHCR is subject to a REFIT (Regulatory Fitness and Performance Programme) evaluation by the European Commission to assess whether the legislation is fit for purpose. Depending on when this exercise is completed it might be interesting to see how it impacts with a potential UK desire to create a food claims system that is more appropriate to UK needs and desires.

CHAPTER SIX
TRACEABILITY, WITHDRAWAL
AND RECALL

Introduction

A food business operator (FBO) may become involved at any time and without warning in a problem concerning food they have received, made or supplied. This can make it a "crisis" for the business, or businesses, involved.

The FBO may be required to act immediately, and may be expected to do so, whether or not they are in any way at fault, if they can intervene to protect consumers.

The way in which the FBO responds will have a direct effect on them and their business. The manner and effectiveness of the response will, to a large extent, be determined by the way in which the FBO is ready to meet the challenges of a food crisis.

This chapter will consider the measures that FBOs should have in place to enable them the meet the challenges of the problem and it will then assess the practical ways in which an FBO can insulate itself from damage.

Types of food crises

The following examples show the wide variety of issues and products that can be involved in a food crisis.

Bacteria

Salmonella (chocolate), listeria (cheese), clostridium botulinum (pâté), campylobacter (chicken salad)

Physical

Plastic/metal (fish cakes), rubber (curry), glass (pasties), moths/larvae (porridge flakes)

Labelling

Undeclared celery (bolognaise bake), undeclared milk (chicken products) incorrect use by dates (meat)

Production

Food produced in unhygienic conditions (sandwiches) or in unapproved premises (meat)

Legal obligations

The two main legal obligations for the purposes of this chapter are contained in Regulation (EC) 178/2002 (the General Food Law Regulation or GFLR); Article 18 concerning traceability and Article 19 setting out the FBOs' responsibilities in respect of unsafe food.

General

The key issues for FBOs are:

- The ability to identify the source of and destination of ingredients and products (traceability);

- Preventing affected foods from reaching consumers (withdrawal);

- Where affected products may have reached consumers telling them about the problem and prevent consumption (consumer information);

- Where other measures will not achieve a high level of public health protection recover affected product from consumers (recall);

- Working with other FBOs and the competent authorities to provide information about the affected product (cooperation and collaboration)

Traceability – Article 18

Article 18 requires FBOs to be able to identify from whom food has been obtained and to whom food has been supplied, and to put in place systems and procedures to allow that information to be provided to the competent authorities.

This is often referred to as the ability to trace products "one-step forward" and "one-step back".

FBOs are not required to have procedures to identify customers when they are the final consumer, although they may need to communicate directly with consumers via retailers or other methods.

Article 18 is worded in terms of its goal and intended result, rather than prescribing how that is to be achieved. In practice, the FBO will adopt a system which records the supplier from whom it obtained the product and the immediate customer along the food to chain to whom it supplies products.

FBOs will use approved suppliers that they have checked, and possibly physically audited, to ensure that the supplier is operating proper procedures.

Problems may arise when FBOs obtain products outside of its approved supplier network. They lose control over the products that enter the food premises and this can introduce uncontrolled hazards which can be the source of a food crisis.

Where FBOs are involved in food manufacture they bring many ingredients into a location and combine them to make intermediate or final products which are then supplied to other FBOs or to final consumers.

FBOs should ensure that they are able to trace how these ingredients are used within their food production operations. This will enable them to quickly identify a suspect ingredient or food, or a particular batch of suspect food. In the event of a food crisis, the FBO may be able to limit the damage if the problem can easily be traced to a particular ingredient or process. This in turn will save time, money and resources.

If this cannot be done quickly and easily and therefore the suspect ingredient may have been used in all the food produced during a specified period, the FBO may need to quarantine and/or destroy a much larger quantity of food. An inability to identify the affected ingredient or product may result in the FBO never quite knowing with any degree of certainty when all the suspect ingredient has been used or removed from production.

The difference between identifying and dealing with one affected batch and with an unknown quantity of suspect food can be hugely significant in terms of FBO resources, loss of customer trust and the reaction of the competent authorities. The inability to be certain about the quantity of affected food may increase the likelihood of legal proceedings (civil and criminal) and the absence of proper documentation will greatly reduce the chances of robustly defending those proceedings.

On the flip side, a good, workable robust traceability system (external and internal) will give the FBO confidence to know that it is doing all it can to minimise the risks of problems arising and that it can react swiftly and effectively in the event that it becomes involved in a food crisis, whether or not of its own making.

Traceability information

Article 18 does not specify precisely what information should be kept but it is generally accepted that this will include:

- Name and address of supplier/customer and identification of the product;

- Date and time of the delivery/other transaction;

- Quantity of product; and

- A reference number or batch code for product in and out

This information must be made available to the competent authority "on demand". It is generally advisable that the information is retained by the FBO for 5 years however this could be much shorter for products with a "use by" or "best before" date.

Each FBO should also have regard to the time limits for various types of legal proceedings and the potential that it may need to rely on records as evidence within those proceedings.

Food of animal origin is subject to specific traceability requirements as set out in Commission Implementing Regulation No 931/2011. The following information must be obtained and upon request provided to the competent authority "without undue delay":

- An accurate description of the food;

- The volume or quantity of the food;

- The name and address of the food business operator from which the food has been dispatched;

- The name and address of the consignor (owner) if different from the food business operator from which the food has been dispatched;

- The name and address of the food business operator to whom the food is dispatched;

- The name and address of the consignee (owner), if different from the food business operator to whom the food is dispatched;

- A reference identifying the lot, batch or consignment, as appropriate; and

- The date of dispatch.

<u>Food Business Operators' responsibilities – Article 19</u>

The starting point for assessing the need to take action is whether the FBO "considers or has reason to believe that a food which it has imported, produced, processed, manufactured or distributed is not in compliance with the food safety requirements".

The FBO's obligation under Article 19 to withdraw food arises when:

1. The food in question is considered unsafe by the operator as not being in compliance with the food safety requirements; and

2. The food is on the market and has left the immediate control of the initial food business.

The reference to food safety requirements is to "unsafe food" as defined in Article 14.

The concept of immediate control is relevant. If all the affected food is identified while still in the food premises (e.g. it has been spotted in the production area or warehouse) and can be quarantined on site, Article 19 obligations may not apply.

That does not mean the situation should be ignored; the FBO will undertake a thorough review of its processes and procedures and take such steps as are necessary to prevent recurrence.

Affected food may be deemed to have left the immediate control of a food business operator when it has been sold or supplied to a wholesaler or it is with any other FBO further along the food distribution chain.

If a FBO considers or has reason to believe that its food is not in compliance with the food safety requirements, and therefore unsafe, and has left its immediate control, what must it do?

- It must immediately initiate procedures to withdraw the food in question and inform the competent authorities;

- If that food may have reached the consumer, the FBO must "effectively and accurately" inform consumers the reason for the withdrawal;

- If the food has been supplied to consumers, the FBO must take such measures to achieve a high level of health protection which may involve recalling those products;

- Where an FBO considers or has reason to believe that a food that it has placed on the market may be "injurious to human health", the FBO must immediately inform the competent authorities of the action taken to prevent risks to the final consumer;

- An FBO must cooperate in actions taken by others and must collaborate with the competent authorities on action to avoid or prevent, reduce or eliminate a risk from the food.

Although withdrawal is not defined in the legislation its purpose is to remove from the food supply chain products which are not actually in the possession of consumers by preventing the distribution, display or offer of an affected product.

Practical application – a typical food crisis

As each situation is unique, there may be no such thing as a "typical" crisis, but the following points may be of general application.

Awareness of a problem

As a food crisis is an unplanned and unexpected event, the FBO cannot predict when a food crisis will happen. Perhaps no more than apocryphally, a food crisis will occur late on a Friday afternoon, near or during holiday periods or when the business is on wind down at the end of a busy week. It may also occur when key members of the crisis management team are away from the business.

The FBO must therefore be ready to respond swiftly and effectively at any time.

The FBO's first response

Don't panic! Now is the time for considered, clear and careful decision-making.

The crisis management plan will have identified the most likely methods of communication with the business in times of crisis. This may be by e-mail, social media, and telephone, or following a visit by officials from the competent authority.

The first person within the business who is likely to be the first to hear about a crisis must be trained to identify an incident which needs an immediate response. This person may be the receptionist, anyone having access to the public e-mail address or anyone monitoring the organisation's social media outlets. The problem may be raised by a staff member who has seen something untoward during production.

Unless the first communication is from the competent authorities, the initial message may not include words such as, "unsafe", "food safety requirement", "withdrawal", "recall", "injurious to health", "unfit for human consumption" or "Article 19 of the General Food Law Regulation"! If the complaint is from a trade customer then the nature of the problem may be clearer.

In the case of an initial communication coming from a consumer the FBO must have trained its staff to identify words or phrases that might require an immediate response in line with the crisis management plan.

How this is done depends on the nature and size of the business. Should all potential food crises be directed immediately to a particular manager or director? In one sense it does not matter to whom the matter is directed as long as they are fully aware of what they need to do next.

Whilst the actual mechanics of the response are business-specific it is essential that some positive action is taken. It would be unacceptable and potentially very damaging for the business, and for consumers, if there is a delay between receipt of the notification and the FBO's first response.

If there is any doubt as to the seriousness of the situation following initial notification, the business may wish to initiate the crisis management procedure. It can always be halted very quickly and the worst-case scenario is staff are left a little red faced if indeed there was no crisis. This is preferable to failing to act and allowing the situation to get out of control.

The FBO's next response

Assuming that the issue has been immediately passed to the relevant in-house person, they need to assess how to respond.

This will involve establishing the full facts. Although this may take a little time it is essential that the correct facts are properly obtained and understood otherwise valuable time, and resources, can be wasted in pursuing a line of enquiry that is not in fact related to the issue of concern.

What information is required?

As much information about the product and the allegation should be obtained.

The initial discussions with the complainant, with the competent authority or with the FBO's own staff will, hopefully, have identified the product and the lot or batch number of which it is a part. This will enable to FBO to interrogate its own records to identify the extent of the problem; when was the product made, which production line was used and can the problem be limited to a single batch or has a significant amount of affected food left the premises.

Next steps

The FBO may need to physically examine the production equipment and/or the maintenance records. It may be necessary to review the production process and check various documents including cooking, cooling, reheating, storage, handling to see if any of these processes are outside the specifications prescribed in the food safety management system. For example, was a product stored at the wrong temperature leading to the growth of harmful pathogens or has a piece of machinery been damaged leading to plastic or metal contaminating food?

Communication

Once the extent of the problem has been properly established the FBO must decide who needs to be aware of the issue and how this is to be done.

This may include; people within the food business and related organisations, the supplier of an affected ingredient, the competent authority and/or downstream customers, retailers and consumers.

How the FBO handles communication to and from relevant stakeholders, including the media, will be highly significant in minimising the impact of the problem for the business and for consumers.

In respect of each communication, the clarity of the message is vital. There is a problem, or a suspected problem, and the FBO must explain what has happened, which product is affected, what is the problem (the hazard and the risk to consumers) and what should people who have purchased the problem do next (i.e. not consume it, return to place of purchase of a full refund etc.).

If the FBO is required to follow the Article 19 procedures, communication with the competent authority should be done as soon as reasonably possible when the FBO is able to provide full information about the extent of the problem and what action it is taking to protect consumers.

In a serious case, it may be necessary to provide initial details to the competent authority while explaining what action the FBO is taking to effectively resolve the situation. Ideally the FBO wants to be the first person to inform the competent authority, or if the authority already knows, the FBO wants to provide reassurance as soon as possible that it has the situation under control.

Even if the FBO is not satisfied that it is required to act under Article 19, there may be merit in telling the competent authority about the problem and outlining what action the FBO is taking.

If the product may have reached consumers the FBO must decide how to inform them of the problem. This may be by way of a recall notice at the point of sale, on a page on the FBO's website, via social media or, in a particularly serious or urgent case by radio or television.

Where the FBO is the manufacturer or producer of the affected product which has been supplied to retailers, it is essential that the retailer is told very clearly what to do and the first FBO needs to be satisfied that the retailer has done what is required to remove the product from the shelves. This will mean doing more than sending an e-mail in the hope that the retailer has read it and has taken the required steps. Following up the e-mail sent to the retailer with a telephone call or personal visit will provide assurance that matters are being dealt with properly.

As the investigation progresses the withdrawal or recall may expand to include other batches of the same product or even new products.

Finalising the issue

It is important that the FBO knows how much affected product has been supplied to retailers, how much has been sold and how much is to be taken off the shelves and returned to the FBO. Inconsistencies or inaccuracies at this stage could lead to affected product remaining on the market with the potential of being consumed.

Once the FBO has dealt with the initial flurry of activity they will have to do a number of things including: undertaking a thorough review and take action to prevent recurrence and/or identify other weaknesses in its systems (possibly reviewing and revising the HACCP system); repairing any reputational damage and restoring consumer confidence; compens-ating consumers or responding to claims for damages and/or being ready to respond to a formal investigation by the competent authorities and being prepared for increased scrutiny from the competent author-ities, suppliers and customers.

A withdrawal or recall is never over until it is over and this only happens when the FBO is satisfied that it has taken all necessary steps to protect consumers and removed affected product from the market.

Crisis management teams and plans

Food business operators should establish crisis management plans and crisis management teams.

The plan will set out the steps to be taken in the event of a food crisis. Staff should be trained to respond in accordance with the plan.

The crisis management team will be determined by the size of the organisation and the extent of its activities but is should include a senior officer who can make decisions including signing off on communications, notifying the competent authority and authorising expenditure. Other members of the team might include the quality director, sales director, heads of the relevant departments, PR adviser (they may be internal or external), food lawyer or food regulatory adviser and someone to make notes and keep a timeline of when key decisions were taken and by whom.

In a cross-border crisis the FBO will need equivalent resources from its representatives or agents in local markets where the affected product has been sold.

The team will need suitable facilities in which to work, including computers and access to refreshments; responding to a crisis may require late night working!

Crisis management plans should be tested and information about crisis management teams should be kept updated (particularly to check that the personnel listed as being part of the team still work with the organisation!).

Conclusion

The FBO will not know how it will respond to a crisis until there is a crisis.

When it does happen, the FBO will, possibly for the first time, be able to assess the effectiveness of their traceability and crisis management procedures.

No one knows how they will react in a crisis but being prepared will instil some degree of confidence in the FBO's ability to respond appropriately. Effective management of a crisis is not something that can be done "on the hoof" by an ill-prepared FBO.

Finally, the FBO must examine its insurance policy to identify what is and what is not covered in the event of them becoming involved in a food crisis requiring withdrawal and/or recall of product and the instruction of appropriate legal and regulatory advisers.

CHAPTER SEVEN
ENFORCEMENT

Introduction

Legislation is only effective if duty-holders comply with it and if it is effectively, transparently and proportionally enforced by the competent authorities. Legislation must therefore be capable of being easily understood and applied by all stakeholders.

This chapter will consider how food law is enforced, short of prosecution, and the following chapters will look at food law as part of the criminal justice system and the regime for sentencing offenders.

The nature of enforcement

EU and national laws, create the framework within which food business operators (FBOs) should carry out their activities and within which competent authorities should carry out inspections and enforcement.

The European Union ensures that the national control systems are effective and working correctly via the Health and Food Audits and Analysis Directorate which carries out inspections and audits in EU Member States and in non-EU countries exporting to the EU. The audits evaluate compliance with EU standards.

That Directorate was previously called the Food and Veterinary Office (FVO) and is part of the Directorate-General for Health and Food Safety (DG Sante).

The EU legislation on official controls is changing and from late 2019 will see Regulation (EU) 2017/625 replace Regulations (EC) No 854/2004 and (EC) No 882/2004 and amend other relevant legislation.

National competent authorities will undertake inspections of food businesses and if they find areas of non-compliance, the competent authority (e.g. a local authority or the Food Standards Agency) must decide on an appropriate and proportionate response.

Principles of enforcement

There are some generally accepted and applicable principles of enforcement which should always be reviewed when advising clients facing enforcement action.

Relevant documents providing guidance on enforcement action include the Food Standards Agency's Food Law Code of Practice (the current version for England is dated March 2017) in conjunction with the Food Law Practice Guidance (the current version for England is dated November 2017), the Manual for Official Controls, the Meat Industry Guide, the Regulator's Code and the Enforcement Policy published by the relevant competent authority.

In relation to how non-compliances will be enforced, those documents include words such as, proportionate, transparent, consistent and risk-based enforcement to reflect the general approach to dealing with non-compliance.

Unless the competent authority, or more specifically the relevant officer on the ground, determines that the breach has created a serious and immediate risk, the authority will often approach the matter by reference to the hierarchy of enforcement.

This might include starting with the least interventionist approach such as taking no action, issuing a warning letter or inspection report, or the authority may believe it is necessary, and proportionate, to escalate matters and serve an enforcement notice or institute criminal proceedings.

Where the competent authority has the power to grant a licence, permit or approval to a food business, the authority may consider a suspension or revocation if the non-compliance is so serious that no lesser method of enforcement will resolve the problem and regularise the situation.

Authorised officers and their powers

Enforcement action, such as issuing enforcement notices, may only be done by an officer who had been duly authorised by the particular competent authority. Checking that the officer has been properly authorised and was authorised at the appropriate time to enforce the particular legislation is an essential first step.

It can often useful to try and establish the officer's level of experience as the issuing of enforcement notices often depends on the relevant officer's opinion based on their assessment of facts they have observed.

The definition of "authorised officer" can be found in the particular legislation and by way of example, Regulation 2 of the Food Safety and Hygiene (England) Regulations 2013 states:

> *""authorised officer", in relation to an enforcement authority, means any person (whether or not an officer of the authority) who is authorised by them in writing, either generally or specially, to act in matters arising under the Hygiene Regulations and Regulation 178/2002;"*

Powers of authorised officers

Once the officer has been properly authorised, they may only act in accordance with powers contained in the legislation under consideration. It is therefore necessary to carefully review that legislation to check that any official action is within the scope of those powers.

For example, Regulation 16 (1) of the 2013 Regulations states:

"An authorised officer of a food authority, on producing, if so required, some duly authenticated document showing authorisation, has a right at all reasonable hours

(a)   *to enter any premises within the authority's area for the purpose of ascertaining whether there is or has been on the premises any contravention of the provisions of the Hygiene Regulations or Regulation 178/2002;*

(b)   *to enter any premises, whether within or outside the authority's area, for the purpose of ascertaining whether there is on the premises any evidence of any such contravention within that area; and*

(c)   *to enter any premises for the purpose of the performance by the authority of their functions under the Hygiene Regulations or Regulation 178/2002,*

but admission to any premises used only as a private dwelling-house may not be demanded as of right unless 24 hours' notice of the intended entry has been given to the occupier."

The same powers are given to an authorised officer of the Food Standards Agency (see Regulation 16 (2)).

Most officials will introduce themselves by reference to their name, occupation (e.g. as an EHO with X Council) and produce some written evidence of their authority. The FBO should not be afraid of asking to see the "duly authenticated document" and the officer should be able to provide this without difficulty. The FBO should make a note of the officer's name.

Entry to premises may also be made under the powers of a court warrant which may be granted if a justice of the peace, on sworn information in writing, is satisfied that the criteria in Regulation 16 (3) are met namely:

1.   There is a reasonable ground for entry for purposes set out in Regulation 16 (1) or 16 (2) and either;

2.   Admission to the premises has been refused, or a refusal is apprehended, and that notice of the intention to apply for a warrant has been given to the occupier; or

3.   An application for admission, or the giving of such notice, would defeat the object of the entry, or the case is one of urgency, or that the premises are unoccupied, or the occupier is temporarily absent.

Reasonable force may be used to gain entry under the power of a warrant.

The FBO, or their representative is given and should retain a copy of the warrant and note any explanation for the entry given by the officers. Making immediate contact with their food law adviser is crucial and in due course the circumstances around the application for and grant of the warrant may be investigated and challenged.

The officer may be accompanied by "such other persons as the officer considers necessary". This may include a police constable or someone with expertise in the matter subject of the investigation.

Once on the premises the officer may do whatever the legislation prescribes which may include:

1.   Inspect records relating to the food business;

2.   Obtain access to a computer where those records are held and to do so may require the assistance of a person in charge of, or using, the computer;

3.   Seize and detain records which the officer has reason to believe may be required as evidence in proceedings under the provisions of the 2013 Regulations; and

4.   In respect of records held electronically, require the records to be produced in a form in which they can be taken away

FBOs require a general awareness of what authorised officers can and cannot do because preventing him or her from carrying out their duties may amount to obstruction (a criminal offence).

Enforcement notices

Food legislation provides a wide variety of enforcement notices that may be issued by authorised officers on behalf of competent authorities.

The form and content of the notice should be checked carefully for compliance with the applicable provisions of the relevant legislation.

In addition, reference should be had to other documents such as the Food Standards Agency's Food Law Code which provides examples of when different types of notices should be used.

Enforcement notices available to competent authorities include:

1.   Improvement Notice (section 10 Food Safety Act 1990 – a very important provision in the context of appeals in respect of various food regulations e.g. food information)

2.   Hygiene Improvement Notice (Regulation 6 of the 2013 Regulations);

3.   Hygiene Emergency Prohibition Notice (Regulation 8 of the 2013 Regulations);

4.   Remedial Action Notice (Regulation 9 of the 2013 Regulations); and

5.   Detention Notice (Regulation 10 of the 2013 Regulations).

The officer issuing the notice must have formed a view about the degree of non-compliance by reference to the provisions of the legislation for example:

1.   If an authorised officer has *reasonable grounds* for believing that the proprietor of a food business is failing to comply with specified regulations (Improvement Notice – IN - section 10 FSA 1990);

2.   If an authorised officer *is satisfied* that the health risk condition is fulfilled with respect to any food business (Hygiene Emergency Prohibition Notice – HEPN - regulation 8 of the 2013 Regulations); and

3.   Where *it appears* to an authorised officer that in respect of premises requiring approval any of the requirements of the Hygiene Regulations is being breached or inspection under the Hygiene Regulations is being hampered (Remedial Action Notice – RAN- regulation 9 of the 2013 Regulations)

In all of these situations the officer must have gathered evidence that justified the appropriate state of mind necessary to issue the notice. If the FBO can show that the officer is wrong about the facts and/or misunderstood them and/or incorrectly applied them in the context of the legislation, there may be grounds for challenging the notice.

Responding to enforcement notices

Failure to comply with an enforcement notice is usually a criminal offence; doing nothing is therefore not usually an option.

In addition to those criminal consequences, receiving an enforcement notice can have very serious consequences for the business. The effect of the notice might be to close the premises until the business has taken some specified action (e.g. with a HEPN the FBO must take action to remove the imminent risk of injury) or the activities may be curtailed (a

RAN may prohibit the use of equipment or the carrying out of any process) and there may be some reputational damage.

How the FBO responds will depend on the circumstances existing at the time. The best course of action may be to comply as quickly as possible and to get the officer to certify that the necessary steps have been taken so the FBO can get back to "business as usual".

The FBO may take some immediate action in response to the notice but may feel sufficiently aggrieved to take matters further. This may be done in accordance with the competent authority's provisions for an internal appeal or it may be done by way of a formal appeal.

Appealing the notice

The notice should explain the mechanism for appealing the notice but the FBO and its advisers should nevertheless check the wording of the legislation, assuming there is a statutory power to appeal the notice, which is not always the case.

The issues to consider include:

1. Is there a statutory power of appeal (if not is it possible to make a claim for judicial review and seek urgent injunctive relief);

2. If there is a statutory power to appeal, the FBO must check certain things; what is the time limit for commencing the appeal, where is the appeal venue (usually the magistrates' court or the First-tier Tribunal - FTT) and what documents are required to commence the appeal;

3. Once the appeal is lodged the FBO needs to know how long before the appeal will be heard. Any delay in the appeal being heard by the court or FTT could have very serious consequences for the food business. If the appeal cannot be heard immediately or within a reasonable time, consideration should be given to

seeking High Court relief to suspend the effect of the notice, at least in the short term.

The following notices may be appealed to the magistrates' court by way of complaint for an order; Hygiene Improvement Notice and Remedial Action Notice (Regulation 22 Food Safety and Hygiene (England) Regulations 2013) and Approval of establishments (Regulation 12 Official Feed and Food Controls (England) Regulations 2009 - refusal to grant, conditional approval withdrawal or suspension of approval).

Appeals to the magistrates' court must usually be commenced within one month of the service of the notice and these appeals come within the civil jurisdiction of the Magistrates' Courts Act 1980. The appeal process commences with the FBO sending a Complaint to the magistrates' court and the appropriate officer will, assuming everything is in order, issue a summons to be served on the respondent competent authority.

The improvement notice procedure under section 10 of the Food Safety Act 1990 has been modified by various pieces of food legislation to provide for an appeal to the FTT against the service of various enforcement notices (see for example the Food Information Regulations 2014, the Fruit Juices and Fruit Nectars (England) Regulations 2013 and the Honey (England) Regulations 2015).

The notice of appeal must be received by the FTT within 28 days of date when the notice/decision was sent to the appellant (as prescribed in the Tribunal Procedure (First-Tier Tribunal) (General Regulatory Chamber) Rule 2009, as amended (the FTT Procedure Rules).

Powers of the Magistrates' Court/First-tier Tribunal

<u>Magistrates' court</u>

The first hearing in the magistrates' court is likely to be used for giving directions for the substantive appeal hearing, the timing of which will depend on issues such as the urgency of the case, court time and availability. Prior to sending the Complaint to the court it can often be prudent to liaise with the court office to establish the likely timeframe for a full hearing at that court or at another court centre.

Evidence of the inability of the court system to accommodate a full hearing within a reasonable period of time will be useful if seeking urgent relief in the High Court.

After hearing the parties and their evidence the magistrates' court "shall make the order for which the complaint is made or dismiss the complaint" (Section 53 (2) Magistrates' Courts Act 1980 - MCA).

First-tier Tribunal

The overriding objective of the FTT Procedure Rules is "to enable the Tribunal to deal with cases fairly and justly" (see rule 2 of the FTT Procedure Rules) and FTT has substantial case management powers to achieve this (see rule 5 of those Rules). The Tribunal will expect the parties to "help the Tribunal to further the overriding objective" and to "co-operate" with the Tribunal (Rule 2).

In an appropriate case, the FTT has the power to suspend the effect of the enforcement notice and such an application should be made within the body of the notice of appeal.

The FTT will send the notice of appeal and accompanying documents to the respondent competent authority and will in due course send the parties a list of directions which may include a suspension of the effect of the notice if this has been requested, and the FTT will ask the parties to provide dates of unavailability within a specified time period to assist in making arrangements for listing the appeal hearing.

Costs

The costs associated with an appeal against an enforcement notice are always a relevant factor for the FBO and for the competent authority.

One issue that needs to be canvassed with the client at the outset is whether, assuming they win, the "loser" will pay their costs.

In the magistrates' court, costs in civil cases, such as these types of appeals, are governed by the provisions of section 64 of the Magistrates'' Courts Act 1980. At the outcome of the appeal the court may make "such order as to costs" as "it thinks just and reasonable" by the "loser" to the "winner".

In the FTT, costs orders are not dependent on "losers" and "winners" as such. Rule 10 of the FTT Procedure Rules states that the Tribunal may make an order for costs only in respect of wasted costs or if the Tribunal considers that a party has acted unreasonably in bringing, defending or conducting the proceedings.

Further appeals

A person aggrieved by the dismissal of an appeal to the magistrates' court, remembering that it has determined the appeal acting in its civil jurisdiction, may appeal to the crown court (see for example, Section 38 Food Safety Act 1990 and Regulation 23 of the 2013 Regulations).

Appeals against a decision of the FTT to the Upper Tribunal are governed by Rule 39 of the FTT Procedure Rules which refer to appeals being brought on a point of law under section 11 of the Tribunals, Courts and Enforcement Act 2007. Permission to appeal to the Upper Tribunal must be sought by way of written application made to the FTT within 28 days of when the FTT sent the decision the subject of the application (Rule 42 of the FTT Procedure Rules).

It should be noted that it is possible to apply to have decisions of the FTT set aside or reviewed.

Conclusion

The key issues for the FBO and their legal advisers are: was the officer duly authorised to issue the notice; did they have the necessary belief, which must be based on evidence, are there sufficient legal grounds for issuing the notice, is the format and content of the notice compliant, is the notice clear in what is alleged to be the non-compliance and in what it requires the recipient to do has it been served properly on the correct legal entity responsible for the alleged non-compliance (i.e. a company or an individual).

Deciding on the response to an enforcement notice is not always straightforward and there is not always an obvious response which may be based, in past, on the consequences of the notice for the FBO.

Whatever decision is taken it should only be reached after a careful assessment of all the options and implications and in doing so, the FBO should work in partnership with its food law advisers and appropriate experts.

CHAPTER EIGHT
CRIMINAL PROSECUTIONS

Introduction

Where food legislation creates criminal offences for non-compliance, those proceedings are subject to the general rules of criminal evidence and procedure including compliance with the Criminal Procedure Rules.

Food offences may be heard in the magistrates' court or in the crown court and the penalties can be very severe (see chapter 9).

Prosecutions are usually taken by competent authorities against the food business operator (FBO) and where the FBO is a company, the law makes provision for proceedings to be taken against the company and, at the same time, against an individual such as a director, manager or similar person where they are responsible for the company's failure to comply with the law.

An individual may therefore be prosecuted because he or she is a director of a corporate FBO or because he or she is an FBO in their own right.

Food law offences

Food legislation will specifically refer to those breaches which create criminal offences and will also set out the maximum penalties (e.g. fines or imprisonment) that may be imposed

The vast majority of food law offences are classed as strict liability offences. The prosecution does not need to prove that the FBO intended to break the law, knew they were breaking the law or was reckless in the manner in which they conducted their activities which led to the contravention. Nevertheless, these issues will be relevant to the sentence that may be imposed.

Reference must be made to the particular piece of legislation under consideration for the precise wording of the offence provisions and for the methods of punishing non-compliance.

The following are two examples based on legislation referred to elsewhere in this book.

Food Safety and Food Hygiene

Regulation 19(1) of the Food Safety and Hygiene (England) Regulations 2013 makes provision for criminal offences.

It states that any person who contravenes or fails to comply with any of the specified EU provisions, as defined, commits an offence.

In practice, the most common offences that come before the court include placing unsafe food on the market (Article 14 of Regulation 178/2002 – see chapter 2) and failing to comply with various hygiene rules contained in Regulations 852/2004 and 853/2004 (see chapter 3).

Food Information

The vast majority of breaches of Food Information Regulations 2014 (FIR) which give national effect to the EU Provision of Food Information to Consumers Regulation (Regulation 1169/2011 – see chapter 4), may only be enforced by means of an improvement notice.

Those breaches of the FIR that attract criminal liability are set out in Regulation 10 and relate to the failure to provide proper allergen information. These offences are summary only meaning that they may only be heard in the magistrates' court although the fine could still be quite significant.

Commencing a criminal prosecution

Criminal prosecutions should only be commenced after a thorough review of the case by the competent authority and its lawyers and where the following questions are answered affirmatively:

1)   Is there enough evidence against the defendant or defendants in respect of each alleged offence?

A criminal case depends on the prosecution adducing sufficient cogent, reliable, credible, admissible evidence to a court that is sufficient to provide a realistic prospect of conviction.

There is either sufficient evidence or there is not. If there is insufficient evidence then the second question should not arise.

2)   Is it in the public interest for the prosecution to bring the case to court?

Once the prosecutor has determined that there is sufficient evidence then all the relevant factors must be weighed in the balance; some pointing towards a prosecution being commenced and some pointing the other way.

Each case is different but some general matters to be taken into account are:

Factors pointing towards prosecution

A serious breach, actual harm or serious risk of harm to the public, significantly misleading consumers, the FBO having previous relevant convictions, the non-compliance having lasted for a long time, particularly in circumstances in which the FBO had been aware of the problem.

Factors pointing against prosecution

A minor breach, a first offence, a one-off set of unforeseeable circumstances not resulting in serious harm or risk of harm, taking swift and effective steps to remedy the problem, personal circumstances (illness, age).

In cases involving breaches of some food legislation it can often be relatively straightforward to show harm or a risk of harm and therefore, in the absence of significant factors against a prosecution, proceedings can usually be justified (whether or not the FBO believes the case to be serious enough to justify a prosecution).

Time limits

Criminal proceedings are usually commenced by the laying of an information at the magistrates' court's office followed by the issue of a summons or by way of a requisition.

The proceedings must be commenced "in time" (i.e. within any statutory limitation period) and this should be checked by the competent authority, the court and by the FBO and their advisers.

The basic principles applicable to time limits are that summary offences (triable only in the magistrates' court), must be commenced within 6 months of the date when the offence was committed although commencing cases that may be tried in the magistrates' court or the crown court is not usually subject to a time limit.

However, some food law offences may be tried in the magistrates' court or the crown court and are subject to specific time limits prescribed in the legislation.

The "usual" situation – time specified in the legislation by reference to the offence

A typical example may be found in Regulation 18 of the 2013 Regulations which states:

> "No prosecution for an offence under these Regulations which is punishable under paragraph (2) of regulation 19 shall be begun after the expiry of—
>
> (a) three years from the commission of the offence; or
>
> (b) one year from its discovery by the prosecutor,
>
> whichever is the earlier."

The impact of a Primary Authority relationship on time limits

Where a food business has entered into a Primary Authority relationship with a local authority this has a, potentially significant, impact on the time period within which criminal proceedings must be commenced.

The relevant legal provisions are to be found in section 28 of the Regulatory Enforcement and Sanctions Act 2008 and related legislation.

The legislation states that an authority seeking to take enforcement action against a business must notify the Primary Authority of its intentions (save in urgent situations not relevant here).

The Primary Authority must consider the proposed enforcement action and review any advice it has given to the business before responding to the enforcing authority which it must do within 5 working days. If the proposed enforcement action can be taken the enforcing authority must inform the business which has 10 working days in which to respond and refer to matter to the Local Better Regulation Office.

During those 15 working days the enforcing authority may not take the proposed enforcement action, which includes prosecution. The practical effect of this is to extend the statutory period within which proceedings must be commenced by those 15 working days.

The FBO should be asked whether it has a Primary Authority relationship and if so this should be taken into account when considering whether the prosecution has been commenced in time.

The investigation and the interview under caution

During the course of it investigation into an alleged breach of food law, the competent authority may invite the FBO or its representative to answer questions about the circumstances of the offence in an interview under caution conducted in accordance with the Police and Criminal Evidence Act 1984 and related Codes of Practice.

This is an important part of the investigation as it allows the competent authority the opportunity to obtain evidence, or further evidence, against the FBO.

It also allows the FBO to put its side of the story and present information to the authority that might persuade it not to prosecute the case.

The FBO should consult their legal adviser to plan the best approach which might be:

1. To attend the interview with their legal adviser and answer all the questions;

2. To attend the interview and submit a prepared statement written under caution and answer no questions;

3. To attend the interview and answer "no comment" to the questions or remain silent; or

4.   To decline to attend the interview but submit a prepared statement under caution setting out the FBO's response to the allegation and providing details of their systems and procedures and explaining what went wrong and setting out the measures it has taken to prevent any recurrence.

There is no "right" response but it is becoming more common for FBOs to cooperate with the investigation by adopting the response at point 4 above.

After the prosecution has been commenced

The business will consider its response to the summons and, having reviewed the prosecution evidence, decide on its plea.

For either way offences where there is no limit on the maximum fine that a magistrates' court can impose, specific listing provisions may apply. Reference should be had to the Criminal Procedure Rules, Practice Directions Division XIII on listing which requires that certain of these offences must be listed before an Authorised District Judge (Magistrates' Court).

Perhaps most common in a food law context are those cases where the defendant corporation has a turnover in excess of £10 million but does not exceed £250 million and has acted in a deliberate, reckless or negligent manner, those cases where the defendant corporation has a turnover in excess of £250 million high profile cases or those where the court will be required to analyse complex company accounts.

Having regard to the court's obligation to apply the Definitive Sentencing Guideline (see chapter 9), the prosecution should be asked, well in advance of the court hearing, to provide a summary of its case including its submissions on issues relevant to the Guideline (most importantly culpability and harm).

It may be possible to agree these in advance of the hearing and for the defendant to prepare a basis of plea (some District Judges require this to be done at the first hearing).

Failure to reach agreement will require the court to make its own assessment based on written and oral submissions or by hearing evidence at a "Newton hearing".

Challenges to the prosecution – due diligence

The FBO may be able to challenge the factual basis for the prosecution case which may include showing gaps in the evidence or showing that the witnesses are wrong.

In addition, the FBO may be able to argue that they did everything that could reasonably have been expected for them to prevent the problem having occurred; the defence of due diligence.

Regulation 12 of the Food Safety and Hygiene (England) Regulations 2013 states that it is a defence for the FBO to prove that they, "took all reasonable precautions and exercised all due diligence to avoid the commission of the offence by the accused or by a person under the control of the accused."

Whether there is any merit in the FBO arguing this defence depends on all the facts and circumstances but, in discussion with their advisers, the following issues may need to be taken into account:

- The food business must have done something to prevent the offence occurring in the first place;

- All reasonable precautions requires the business to put in place a sufficient and robust food safety management system to prevent what allegedly happened from happening (see the earlier discussions around this and HACCP);

- All due diligence means that the business has put in place a sufficient and robust procedures of checking to ensure that the system is working correctly and to make appropriate changes if it is not;

- The systems and procedures should be written down and staff must be trained on them;

- Documents and records must be maintained;

- The systems and procedures must be capable of proactively preventing problems and reactively correcting them when required;

- Allocation of responsibilities in respect of the systems and procedures must be recorded;

- The systems and procedures must cover all aspects of the food business;

- The systems and procedures relied on for the due diligence defence must relate to the offence or offences before the court.

Where the FBO seeks to blame someone else for the offence they must provide the prosecutor with information "identifying or assisting in the identification" of that other person (Regulation 12 (5)).

The FBO will need to present evidence about its business and its systems and may require an expert to comment on them in light of what was in place and operating and, perhaps, to advise the court about the standards that are to be expected and the extent to which the FBO was complying with those standards.

The ideal expert is someone with perhaps four key qualities:

1. A sound knowledge and understanding of the particular sector and the topic under consideration;

2.   The ability to write a thorough, well-researched report dealing with the issues;

3.   The ability to explain that report and complex scientific evidence in a simple, straightforward and easy to understand manner; and

4.   Has the confidence to say when something is outside their area(s) expertise and not get dragged in to discussing matters best left to others.

The final prerequisite for any expert is an understanding of the role and duties of the expert which are to "give opinion which is objective and unbiased" and which is "within the expert's area or areas of expertise" (see Criminal Procedure Rules 2015, Part 19 – similar provisions relating to experts can be found in Part 35 of the Civil Procedure Rules).

Above all, the expert owes a duty to the court and not to the person paying his or her fee.

Conclusion

As most food law offences are strict liability there may provide little opportunity to successfully defend them. This does not mean that the FBO should not, where appropriate, challenge the prosecution case.

However, if the FBO has put in place proper procedures and systems and these are functioning correctly it may be possible to show that there was not much else they could have done to comply with their obligations and the contravention occurred despite all these measures being in place.

This may have three consequences; it may deter the competent authority from bringing a criminal prosecution, it may allow the FBO to argue the due diligence defence and it may be very relevant to any sentence that the court may impose.

CHAPTER NINE
SENTENCING

Introduction

The "Health and Safety Offences, Corporate Manslaughter and Food Safety and Hygiene Offences – Definitive Guideline" took effect on 1st February 2016 and the result has been a significant change in the way in which the parties and the courts approach sentencing in food law cases.

The Guideline was introduced in England and Wales because of a perception that sentences in food safety and hygiene cases were quite low, coupled with inconsistencies between different courts. This inconsistent approach made it hard to advise food businesses operators on the likely level of punishment.

The general impression is that penalties for food law offences subject to the Guideline have increased since February 2016, particularly so for large organisations having a substantial turnover.

The Guideline may not have removed the perceived previous inconsistent sentences, but it has allowed all parties, the prosecution, the FBO and the court, to standardise, to a degree, the way in which sentencing hearings are conducted.

This chapter will focus on the approach to sentencing required by the Guideline, although it does not apply to all food law offences committed in England and Wales.

The Guideline – general issues

Food law offences subject to the provisions of the Guideline include some of the matters referred to elsewhere in this book namely; placing unsafe food on the market, breaches of hygiene legislation, non-compliance with traceability requirements and breaches of the provisions regarding withdrawal and recall of unsafe foods.

Before looking at the Guideline in detail it should be noted that the law is slightly different between England and Wales.

In England the law on safety and hygiene has been combined in the Food Safety and Hygiene (England) Regulations 2013 whereas in Wales the law remains divided; the General Food Regulations 2004 and the Food Hygiene (Wales) Regulations 2006.

This has little impact when an organisation is being sentenced in that the corporate FBO faces an unlimited fine.

Under the 2013 England Regulations, an FBO who is an individual and is being sentenced by the magistrates' court may not be sent to prison; he or she may only be fined. In a particularly serious case, the inability of the magistrates' court to impose a custodial sentence may mean the case is sent to the crown court to be dealt with although this does not mean a prison sentence will be imposed.

In Wales an individual being sentenced in the magistrates' court for a food safety offence, and also for offences relating to traceability, withdrawal and recall, may be sent to prison for a term up to 6 months.

In both jurisdictions, the crown court may impose a maximum punishment of 2 years' imprisonment.

Although the Guideline provides a structured approach that the parties and the court must follow, it remains flexible enough to allow the court to have regard to all the relevant factors and impose a sentence that is appropriate in all the circumstances (for example see the comments at paragraph 12 in the case of *Whirlpool Appliances v Regina (HSE) [2017] EWCA Crim 2186*, as applied in *R (HSE) v ATE Truck and Trailer Sales Limited* [2018] EWCA Crim 752).

Sentencing of organisations

The Guideline clearly sets out how the structured approach is to apply but the following points are particularly relevant.

<u>Step One – determining the offence category</u>

The court must determine the offence category "using only the culpability and harm factors" that are set out on page 30 of the Guideline.

Culpability

There are 4 levels of culpability; very high, high, medium and low.

Category	Applicability
Very High	The most serious cases where there has been "a deliberate breach of or flagrant disregard for the law".
High	Offender fell far short of the appropriate standard (e.g. failing to put proper measures in place, allowing breaches to go on for a long time, serious/systematic failure to address risks to health and safety)
Medium	Offender fell short of the appropriate standard (e.g. systems were in place but not sufficiently adhered to or implemented)
Low	Offender did not fall far short of the appropriate standard (e.g. significant efforts to secure food safety, minor failings occurred as an isolated incident)

It is usually clear where a case is "very high" or "low" but the parties must carefully assess all the evidence to either agree whether the case is "high" or "medium" or to clearly set out their rival submissions for the benefit of the court.

Harm

Harm factors include actual harm and a risk of harm which involves a consideration of likelihood of harm and the extent of the harm if it does occur.

Death is not specifically mentioned as a harm factor. In its consultation document which preceded the Definitive Guideline, the Sentencing Council, stated that serious harm, including death, arising from food cases was a potential outcome this was, in practice, rare. Where death or very serious injury does occur, the court would be entitled to reflect this by moving outside the category range.

There are three categories of harm: 1, 2 and 3.

Category	Applicability
1	Serious adverse effects on individual(s) and/or having a widespread impact. High risk of an adverse effect on individual(s) including a supply to vulnerable groups.
2	Adverse effect on individual(s) not amounting to category 1. Medium risk of an adverse effect or low risk of a serious adverse effect. Regulator and/or legitimate industry substantially undermined.

	Relevant authorities unable to trace products or are otherwise inhibited in identifying or addressing risks to health. Consumer mislead regarding food's compliance with religious or personal beliefs.
3	Low risk of an adverse effect on individual(s). Public misled about the specific food consumed, but little or no risk of actual adverse effect on individuals.

Again, the parties may be able to agree the appropriate category but if not, the court will need clear submissions supported by evidence, possibly expert evidence, to assist it make a determination.

Step 2 – Starting point and category range

The starting point fine is based on the organisation's annual turnover, or equivalent, and hence the provision of accounts to the court is crucial. Usually the court will want to see three years' accounts in order to get a true picture of the organisation's financial situation.

If accounts are not produced or the court has doubt about the financial information that has been provided the court may infer that the organisation can pay any fine.

Although the court should only have regard to the financial situation of the organisation being sentenced, it may have regard to the resources of a "linked organisation" where they "can properly be taken into account" (see *Regina v Tata Steel UK Limited* [2017] EWCA Crim 704).

The Guideline contains four tables of fines based on the organisation's turnover:

- Large – turnover £50 million and over

- Medium – turnover between £10 million and £50 million

- Small – turnover between £2 million and £10 million

- Micro – turnover not more than £2 million

Organisations with a turnover that "greatly exceeds the threshold for large organisations" may, but not must, require the court to increase the fine to "achieve a proportionate sentence".

This does not mean that the court simply decides on a level of fine in the appropriate table and applies a multiplier based on the amount by which the turnover exceeds the £50 million figure for a "large" organisation (see *Whirlpool Limited* at paragraph 34).

When representing a very large organisation, careful thought must be given to explaining to the judge, if necessary, why she or he should not significantly increase the level of fine *just because* the organisation has an exceptionally large turnover.

Within each of the four tables the Guideline provides a starting point fine and a range of fines.

By way of example:

In respect of a large organisation where the court's assessment of the case is high culpability with harm category 2, the starting point fine is £230,000.00 with a category range of between £90,000.00 and £600,000.00.

For a small organisation where the assessment of the case is high culpability and harm category 2, this attracts a starting point fine of £24,000.00 with a range between £8,000.00 and £90,000.00.

Some of the factors relevant to moving up or down the category range are found on page 34 of the Guideline.

Factors increasing seriousness (and hence inviting a move upwards from the starting point fine include: previous convictions (made worse if of a similar nature and are recent), motivated by financial gain, deliberately concealing the offence, a poor safety or hygiene record and, perhaps interestingly, refusal of free advice or training (a point mentioned in chapter 3 in connection with the resources available to FBOs in respect of setting up food safety management systems and HACCP).

Factors reducing seriousness (and hence inviting a move downwards from the starting point) include; the absence of relevant recent convictions, steps taken to voluntarily remedy the problem, a good food safety and hygiene record, cooperation and acceptance of responsibility.

Step 3 – step back

Having applied the above factors and arrived at a fine, the court must "step back" and have regard to the objectives of sentencing in order to assess whether the fine, which has been heavily influenced by the organisation's turnover and the above factors, is "proportionate to the overall means of the offender".

Sentencing should have regard to the need for punishment, deterrence and the removal of gain obtained from the illegal activity (something different to a formal application under proceeds of crime legislation).

A long-standing feature of sentencing in food and other regulatory cases, requires that the fine has a "real economic impact" on the organisation to send a message to "both management and shareholders".

It goes without saying that senior representatives of the organisation with responsibility for food and regulatory compliance, including those at board level, should attend the sentencing hearing. This shows the court that the organisation takes the matter very seriously and the judge's sentencing remarks will be heard directly by those responsible for the organisation's activities.

The following will be relevant to assessing whether and adjustment is required:

- Profit margin – where the organisation has a high turnover but operates consistently with a small profit margin, this may lead to a downwards adjustment of the fine (the opposite will of course apply where the organisation has a high profit margin);

- Economic benefit from the offence – this might be a quantifiable sum of money gained from the non-compliance but it might include costs saved by not doing what was required or other savings;

- Putting the organisation out of business – the court will bear in mind that a high fine might result in the organisation closing with the loss of direct and indirect jobs. While the court is reluctant to impose a fine having that effect, this may be inevitable in a particularly bad case;

The Guideline allows the court to impose a large fine, to reflect the seriousness of the offence, but to require it to be paid "if necessary over a number of years".

<u>Step Four – other factors</u>

This step requires the court to have regard to the particular effect of a fine on public or charitable bodies.

If the organisation can show that the fine would have a "significant impact" on the provision of their services, the Guideline suggest that the fine should "normally be substantially reduced".

The organisation must provide some evidence of the impact, or likely impact, of a large fine. The court can consider anything that is relevant including the wider impact of a fine on the employment of staff, service users, customers and local economy.

However, the Guideline makes it clear that at step four the court is concerned with the impact of a fine on the organisation's ability to provide valuable, or sometimes essential, services. The impact of the fine on shareholders and/or directors is not to be taken into account.

Step Five – assistance to the prosecution

This step is very specific and goes well over and beyond the expected level of cooperation which is a mitigating factor at step two.

Step five applies to sections 73 and 74 of the Serious Organised Crime and Police Act 2005 and any other rule of law by which a defendant may receive a discounted sentence "in consequence of assistance given (or offered) to the prosecutor or investigator".

This is unlikely to apply in the vast majority of food law cases.

However, it may have a role to play in a particularly complex and large-scale food poisoning or misdescription case where the information assists in providing information about other participants and helps to protect consumers, thus saving the investigators a significant amount of time and resources.

Step Six – reduction for a guilty plea

As we saw earlier, fines in food cases can be very high and the reduction in sentence following a guilty plea can be quite significant. Where the guilty plea is entered at a very early stage in the legal proceedings the FBO can reasonably expect the fine to be reduced by one-third.

Where a guilty plea is entered at later stages of the proceedings the reduction may only be one-quarter and if the guilty plea is tendered at trial, there may be no reduction at all.

In this regard reference should be made to the Reduction in Sentence for a Guilty Plea Guideline (see below).

<u>Step Seven – compensation and ancillary matters</u>

The court will consider whether to order the defendant to pay compensation to one or more victims of the offence and it may also prohibit the defendant from being involved in the management of a food business (see below).

<u>Step 8 – Totality principle</u>

Where a defendant is to be sentenced for more than one offence, as is nearly always the case in food matters, the court must ensure that the overall penalty is just and proportionate (see below).

<u>Step 9 – Reasons</u>

When imposing its sentence, the court is required to give reasons for its decision. This is an important part of the process and can help a defendant identify whether the court may have erred in its application of the law, the facts, and the sentencing guideline, or in any other way.

Sentencing of Individuals

The Guideline applies to individuals and is based on the same general approach to the sentencing of organisations.

<u>Step One – offence category</u>

The court applies the factors to determine the offence category by reference to culpability and harm.

Culpability

The same four categories apply to the sentencing of individuals: very high, high, medium and low.

Category	Applicability
Very high	Intentional breach or flagrant disregard for the law
High	Actual foresight of, or wilful blindness to, risk of offending but risk is nevertheless taken
Medium	Offence committed through act or omission which a person exercising reasonable care would not commit.
Low	Offence committed with little fault (significant, but inadequate, efforts to address the risk; no warning indicating a risk to food safety; minor failings and an isolated incident

Harm

The categories of harm are similar to those applicable to the sentencing of organisations and similar issues arise with regard to the sentencing of individuals.

Step Two – starting point and category range

In order to provide the court with details of his or her finances, the defendant will be required to complete a form entitled "statement of assets and other financial circumstances". The court can require an individual to provide further information to corroborate the figures set out on the form and may require evidence of this to be given under oath.

If no information is provided or the court is not satisfied that it has been given sufficient reliable information, it may draw the inference that the defendant can pay any fine.

Having assessed the levels of culpability and harm, the court will consider whether a term of imprisonment is appropriate.

Alternatively, the court may impose a fine which is based on a percentage of the individual's relevant weekly income (see below).

The court may decide to impose a punishment between a fine and imprisonment, or it may decide not to impose a penalty.

However, where a custodial sentence is a potential outcome, the Guideline requires the court to ask itself the following questions:

1.   Has the custody threshold been passed?

2.   If so, is it unavoidable that a custodial sentence be imposed?

3.   If so, can that sentence be suspended?

The court may also consider imposing a community penalty, the requirements of which aim to punish offenders, to change offenders' behaviour so they don't commit crime in the future, and to make amends to the victim of the crime or the local community. This might include performing a specified number of hours of unpaid work.

Where this is a potential sentence, the court must ask itself whether the community threshold has been passed and event if it has the Guideline suggests that a fine will "normally be the most appropriate disposal".

Practitioners should refer to the Sentencing Council's document, Imposition of Community and Custodial Sentences, Definitive Guideline which took effect on 1st February 2017.

This document is very helpful in considering the thresholds for the imposition of community orders and custodial sentences, and also provides a list of the fine bands.

These are based on a percentage of relevant weekly income (RWI), as defined, and range from Band A (starting point 50% of RWI with a range of 25-75% of RWI) to Band F (starting point 600% of RWI with a range of 500-700% of RWI).

Step two also includes a list of aggravating factors and mitigating factors, some of which mirror those applicable to the sentencing of organisations.

Additional mitigating factors relevant to individuals that might be deployed in an appropriate case include:

• Good character and/or exemplary conduct;

• Mental disorder or learning disability where linked to the commission of the offence;

• Serious medical conditions requiring urgent, intensive or long-term treatment;

• Age and/or lack of maturity where it affects the responsibility of the offender; and

• Sole or primary care for dependent relatives.

As with all other issues relating to sentencing hearings, the court will expect to receive evidence from the defendant, and from the prosecution, before it can, or should, properly take any matters into account.

Step Three – Review the financial element of the sentence

As required by the general principles of sentencing, the court will have regard to the seriousness of the offence and the defendant's financial circumstances.

Step Four - Assistance to the prosecution

The court will apply the same principles as set out above as they apply to organisations.

Step Five – Reduction for Guilty Pleas

See below

Step Six – Compensation and ancillary orders

See below.

Step Seven – Totality

See below.

Step Eight – Reasons

See above.

Step Nine

The court must consider giving credit for time spent on bail.

Some points applicable to the sentencing of organisations and individuals

Guilty Plea

It is well known that a defendant will receive a lesser sentence after pleading guilty in a criminal case.

Although there may be a substantial financial advantage for a client to enter a guilty plea, it should only be done after very careful consideration of all the relevant factors, where there are no viable defences and where the prosecution has provided sufficient admissible evidence to prove that the client has committed the particular offence, or offences.

Since 1st June 2017 the Reduction in Sentence for a Guilty Plea Definitive Guideline must be applied.

The Guilty Plea Guideline provides a very clear approach to dealing with a reduction in sentence for a guilty plea:

Stage 1: Determine the appropriate sentence for the offence(s) in accordance with any offence- specific sentencing guideline.

Stage 2: Determine the level of reduction for a guilty plea in accordance with this guideline.

Stage 3: State the amount of that reduction.

Stage 4: Apply the reduction to the appropriate sentence.

Stage 5: Follow any further steps in the offence specific guideline to determine the final sentence.

For present purposes, stage 2 is of particular relevance; how much of a reduction will the court award.

The Guilty Plea Guideline states the following:

1.   The maximum reduction for a guilty plea is one-third;

2.   Guilty plea indicated at the first stage of proceedings – one-third reduction;

3.   Guilty plea indicated after the first stage of proceedings – one-quarter reduction decreasing to a maximum of one-tenth reduction on the first day or trial;

4.   Guilty plea entered during trial – may justify a zero reduction.

An issue can arise as to what amounts to "the first stage of proceedings" and when this occurs in a particular case. The Guideline indicates that this will "normally be the first hearing at which a plea or indication of plea is sought and recorded by the court".

From the perspective of an individual, the reduction of a sentence following a guilty plea might have the following consequences in addition to a reduction in the quantum of the sentence:

1.   A custodial sentence might become a community sentence;

2.   A community sentence might become a fine;

3.   The case might remain in the magistrates' court (noting the limitation on the imposition of custodial sentences by a magistrates' court).

<u>Compensation and ancillary orders</u>

Compensation

The court will consider whether to award compensation to the victim of an offence who has suffered loss or damage. If it does so then the payment of compensation takes precedence over the payment of any other financial penalty where the defendant's means are limited.

Courts are generally reluctant to award compensation other than in simple and straightforward cases where the amount can easily and readily be ascertained. While this was, and has been, the generally accepted approach, courts more willing to entertain applications for compensation in a broader spectrum of cases, for example where the victim's only realistic chance of receiving compensation was through the criminal courts, there was no recompense by virtue of an insurance policy and/or if there was an ineffective remedy in civil proceedings.

In a food case the court may be willing to entertain a claim for compensation in a food poisoning claim and if so the judge might refer to the Judicial Studies Board's "Guidelines for the Assessment of General Damages in Personal Injury Cases".

Hygiene Prohibition Order (HPO)

Following conviction for an offence the Food Safety and Hygiene (England) Regulations 2013, and its Welsh equivalent, the court may "impose a prohibition on the food business operator participating in the management of any food business".

The Regulations specify that the court may impose such a hygiene prohibition order where it thinks it is "proper to do so in all the circumstances of the case.

This may be because of the general poor hygiene record and/or a history of failing to heed warnings or advice and/or the court has little confidence that the defendant will comply fully with legal obligations in the future. Furthermore, the court will have regard to the deterrent effect of a HPO to send a powerful message to others working in the food industry that they must comply strictly with the requirements of rigorous food hygiene.

An HPO may be made against an individual and a corporate defendant.

Director's disqualification

Where a person is convicted of an indictable offence in connection with the promotion, formation, management of a company, and other specified company related activities, (which includes all food offences of that description whether or not they are within the ambit of the Sentencing Guideline), the court may order that the person may not be a director of a company or whether directly or indirectly be involved in the management of a company.

Such an order is there to protect the public from people who, for reasons of dishonesty, or naivety or incompetence, abuse their role and status as director. The period of disqualification is up to 15 years when the person is sentenced in the crown court (the maximum is 5 years in the magistrates' court).

Totality principle

Where a court is sentencing a defendant in respect of more than one offence the court determines the sentence for each offence and then assesses whether the total sentence is just and proportionate.

If, having regard to all matters the court thinks that it is then the aggregate sentence remains.

If not, the court has a number of options to arrive at a just and proportionate total sentence:

1.   For offences committed on the same occasion, the court may impose a fine for one offence (usually the most serious offence) and then in respect of the other offences, reduce what would otherwise be the sentence for other offences or impose no separate penalty;

2.   For offences committed on more than one occasion, the court may consider imposing a mixture of consecutive and concurrent sentences.

Prosecution costs

The defendant will be required to pay the costs of the prosecution to the extent that they are "just and reasonable" – section 18 of the Prosecution of Offenders Act 1985. The prosecution should produce a breakdown of its costs and this should be made available to the defendant at the sentencing hearing, if not beforehand.

The court does not tend to determine costs in the same detailed manner as might be found in a civil case, but the court may require an explanation of how the costs have been incurred by the prosecution (including legal, investigative and experts' fees).

Having been supplied with the prosecution's costs breakdown, it is commonplace for there to be an agreement between the parties as to the amount of costs that the defendant agrees to pay.

In a complex case, even following a guilty plea, the prosecution's costs can be high, possibly in the tens of thousands of pounds, and so the defendant should carefully review the costs schedule and, where appropriate, make submissions to the court on those aspects which the FBO does not believe are "just and reasonable".

Pragmatism has a part to play because if the court needs to consider costs in detail this may require an additional hearing and the costs of that hearing might outweigh the potential saving for the defendant.

Victim surcharge

When the court imposes a sentence, it must also make provision for the payment of the appropriate victim surcharge which is used to fund victim support services.

Time to pay

Once the court has made a final determination on the payment of fines, compensation (if any) and costs, it will make an order for the payment of the total amount. The court may require the amount to be paid immediately or it may allow a period of time (for example 14 or 28 days) in which the total sum must be paid.

If, after the hearing, the defendant gets into difficulty in paying the financial penalty contact should be made with the court office otherwise the court might take steps to enforce payment.

Imprisonment in default

Where the crown court imposes a fine the judge must also specify a maximum period of imprisonment in default of payment of the fine.

Proceeds of crime

In an appropriate case the defendant might face an application under the proceeds of crime legislation to remove financial gain achieved through criminality.

Conclusion

Sentencing of food cases is now subject to the step by step approach envisaged by the Guideline although, in order to reach a just and proportionate sentence, the Guideline should not be followed rigidly.

However, it is crucial that all parties have regard to those pieces of evidence that have particular relevance to the court's determination of the appropriate sentence. The prosecution and defence should produce written submissions setting out their respective positions, in advance of the hearing.

This may involve them collaborating or setting out where they agree and disagree in an attempt to assist the court and save time and resources (in this regard see the observations at paragraph 51 in the case of *R (Health and Safety Executive) v ATE Truck & Trailer Sales Ltd* [2018] [2018] EWCA Crim 752.

Where agreement cannot be reached, the court will decide if it can properly sentence the defendant based on the written material or whether evidence needs to be heard.

CHAPTER TEN
CONCLUSION WITH A COMMENT ABOUT BREXIT!

We hope this book has stayed true to its brief; a user-friendly practical guide to food law.

There are many topics that could have been included; GMOs, novel food, food contact materials, animal welfare for instance and some of the content could have been expanded on; non-statutory labelling (claims regarding "natural" etc.), origin labelling and related issues such as advertising to name a few.

One subject which has been mentioned briefly but could have been allocated a chapter in its own right is Brexit.

With less than a year to go until the UK leaves the EU, albeit followed by a transitional period, many issues and fears around the future exist.

From an agri-food perspective there are many challenges which may affect FBOs and consumers alike.

Will the UK be part of the, or a, Customs Union (e.g. affecting the free movement of goods), the implications of the UK being a third country (e.g. labelling of the name and address for food information purposes and health and identification marking of foods), what food labelling rules will apply and how will they be interpreted and applied (e.g. mandatory labelling and GMOs) and will the UK begin a plan of divergence to make food laws more "UK-relevant" or "UK-friendly" (e.g. animal welfare rules, food composition, nutrition and health claims and labelling)?

Leaving the EU will create opportunities for some FBOs, both within and outside the UK, and indeed for the UK as a nation, but great care must be taken to avoid a wide gap between the regulatory requirements in the UK and its close trading partners (for example dual labelling of foods for sale in the UK and in the EU).

Brexit is well rehearsed in the media and within sector-specific groups and nothing can be taken for granted except for one thing; there will be change. It is the extent to which this will happen which is causing concern and consternation.

It might be useful to reflect on the food industry during the change of food labelling law from the general labelling provisions in Directive 2000/13/EC to Regulation 1169/2011 (EUFIC). The Regulation came into force in late 2011 with an implementation date for most of its provisions set for December 2014 with the mandatory nutrition declaration provisions coming onto force in December 2016).

It was very clear that most, if not all, food labels would need to be changed. For some FBOs these changes were planned well in advance of the deadline and revamping labels was often incorporated into a general business strategy involving and brand review and was, for some, a good excuse for new marketing strategies.

For some food business operators, the changes were left to the last minute and hence some positive opportunities were lost and some FBOs were selling non-compliant product (even having regard to the transitional positions).

In due course all, or nearly all, FBOs changed their labels and not much was lost for them or their businesses.

There is a very real concern that not being fully prepared for Brexit will lead to much more serious consequences for particular sectors of the food industry, for individual FBOs and ultimately for consumers.

Each FBO should consider how their particular activities and operations *might* be affected by Brexit. This might happen in several different ways.

Sourcing ingredients might become harder and/or more expensive, with all the obvious consequences that flow from this, and it may become more difficult to obtain suitably qualified and experienced staff.

It may be useful for FBOs to identify alternative suppliers, some inside and some outside the UK and the EU. If one ingredient becomes harder to obtain or more expensive, might this result in prices rises or it may require a reformulation of a product or product line.

The time to review the possible impact of Brexit is now; other FBOs are doing so and it would be very unfortunate if on the appointed day, or beforehand (even having regard to the transitional provisions) an FBO was unable to obtain the ingredients it needs or they became subject to some sort of tariff or quota as a result of the mammoth negotiating process that the UK needs to undertake.

There is no justification for burying one's head in the sand and, although preparation is essential, the process need not be so over-whelming as to be impossible.

Brexit is likely to cause hardship, possibly severe hardship, to some but it will also create opportunities for others, possibly in terms of new product development, opening new markets or refocussing on specific areas of the food business.

To "borrow" a well-known phrase to highlight the importance of being aware of the consequences of Brexit, "Preparation Prevents Poor Per-formance" or turned on its head; lack of preparation for those consequences could mean the end of a business that has taken years to develop.

There are wider issues of concern that need to be considered such as food safety and the implications of reduced border checks, and fewer inspections elsewhere in the food system, leading to increased risks of dangerous food on the market, leading to increased chances of illness and death, leading to mistrust of food providers, leading to reduced food security leading to shortages of certain foods and implications for health and nutrition.

Is this scaremongering? Possibly, but from little changes flow big consequences and when these are not fully appreciated by everyone with an interest in food (i.e. every single one of us whether as politicians, regulators, authorities, food business operators, food law practitioners and consumers) the risk of adverse consequences increases, at least in the very important short term.

Brexit creates uncertainty; businesses, and to some extent, consumers want to avoid uncertainty.

Nevertheless, food law is, and will continue to be, a fascinating, and relevant, subject from so many different perspectives.

MORE BOOKS BY
LAW BRIEF PUBLISHING

A selection of our other titles available now:

'Occupiers, Highways and Defective Premises Claims: A Practical Guide Post-Jackson – 2nd Edition' by Andrew Mckie
'A Practical Guide to Financial Ombudsman Service Claims' by Adam Temple & Robert Scrivenor
'A Practical Guide to the Law of Enfranchisement and Lease Extension' by Paul Sams
'A Practical Guide to Marketing for Lawyers – 2nd Edition' by Catherine Bailey & Jennet Ingram
'A Practical Guide to Advising Schools on Employment Law' by Jonathan Holden
'Certificates of Lawful Use and Development: A Guide to Making and Determining Applications' by Bob Mc Geady & Meyric Lewis
'A Practical Guide to the Law of Dilapidations' by Mark Shelton
'A Practical Guide to the 2018 Jackson Personal Injury and Costs Reforms' by Andrew Mckie
'A Guide to Consent in Clinical Negligence Post-Montgomery' by Lauren Sutherland QC
'A Practical Guide to Running Housing Disrepair and Cavity Wall Claims: 2nd Edition' by Andrew Mckie & Ian Skeate
'A Practical Guide to the General Data Protection Regulation (GDPR)' by Keith Markham
'A Practical Guide to Digital and Social Media Law for Lawyers' by Sherree Westell
'A Practical Guide to Holiday Sickness Claims – 2nd Edition' by Andrew Mckie & Ian Skeate
'A Practical Guide to Inheritance Act Claims by Adult Children Post-Ilott v Blue Cross' by Sheila Hamilton Macdonald
'A Practical Guide to Elderly Law' by Justin Patten

'A Practical Approach to Clinical Negligence Post-Jackson' by Geoffrey Simpson-Scott
'A Practical Guide to Personal Injury Trusts' by Alan Robinson
'Employers' Liability Claims: A Practical Guide Post-Jackson' by Andrew Mckie
'A Practical Guide to Subtle Brain Injury Claims' by Pankaj Madan
'The Law of Driverless Cars: An Introduction' by Alex Glassbrook
'A Practical Guide to Costs in Personal Injury Cases' by Matthew Hoe
'A Practical Guide to Alternative Dispute Resolution in Personal Injury Claims – Getting the Most Out of ADR Post-Jackson' by Peter Causton, Nichola Evans, James Arrowsmith
'A Practical Guide to Personal Injuries in Sport' by Adam Walker & Patricia Leonard
'The No Nonsense Solicitors' Practice: A Guide To Running Your Firm' by Bettina Brueggemann
'Baby Steps: A Guide to Maternity Leave and Maternity Pay' by Leah Waller
'The Queen's Counsel Lawyer's Omnibus: 20 Years of Cartoons from The Times 1993-2013' by Alex Steuart Williams

These books and more are available to order online direct from the publisher at www.lawbriefpublishing.com, where you can also read free sample chapters. For any queries, contact us on 0844 587 2383 or mail@lawbriefpublishing.com.

Our books are also usually in stock at www.amazon.co.uk with free next day delivery for Prime members, and at good legal bookshops such as Hammicks and Wildy & Sons.

We are regularly launching new books in our series of practical day-to-day practitioners' guides. Visit our website and join our free newsletter to be kept informed and to receive special offers, free chapters, etc.

You can also follow us on Twitter at www.twitter.com/lawbriefpub.